tell in the wilderness

*

tell in the wilderness

*

M A X   W A R R E N

The Highway Press

6 SALISBURY SQUARE · LONDON E.C.4
1959

Printed in Great Britain by
Wyman & Sons, Limited, London, Fakenham and Reading

AUTHOR'S NOTE

In the   mmer of 1958 I was commissioned to write the
C.M.S. Book of the Year' round the theme 'The Christ
we proclaim'. In preparation for this I canvassed a large
number of missionaries, sending to them an outline of the
kind of book I would like to write if they would help me.
The response was wonderfully generous. More than that,
it was an exciting response. The courageous clearsighted-
ness, the very deep humility, the invincible hopefulness,
which their letters expressed afforded a spiritual experience
I will not soon forget. I can only pray that in the reading
of this book some will be able to share in it.

In their replies a number of those missionaries were kind
enough to say that they would be praying that the writing
of the book would be a joyful undertaking. Before reading
what they had written I was in anything but a joyful frame
of mind! But those prayers were answered, thanks to the
generosity with which the writers gave themselves, yes,
revealed themselves. With them I too was able to find in
the wilderness 'the mountain of God'.

This 'Book of the Year', in its immediate form, is a
picture of C.M.S. at work in the persons of its missionaries.
But inextricably intermingled with them, as the reader will
discover, are men and women of other races who represent
the growing company of Christ's faithful people all over the
world. In the deepest sense of the word this book has no
local or limited reference at all. That is why the initials
C.M.S. appear only in this preface.

Having said 'thank you' to the missionaries who provided
the material for this book let me also add a word of gratitude
to Miss Greta Preston who sorted and arranged all the
replies with meticulous care and imagination: to Miss
Jennings and Miss Jennison who under great pressure of

time did the typing: and to Miss Glynne Evans who as
Editor dealt faithfully with me, and who yet must be held
innocent of all blame for anything which may be thought
amiss.

"Lo, here is fellowship"

M. A. C. W.

*All the quotations from Scripture are given in the Revised
Standard Version.*

Prologue

Moses . . . led his flock to the west side of the wilderness, and came to Horeb, the mountain of God.   EXODUS 3. 1.

Did Moses just happen to be that way with his sheep and goats? Or had he a purpose that day? Was he expecting that something would happen, something to which he could hardly give a name? Was there some premonition in his mind that he was going to meet Someone, hear a voice, have a revelation? We do not know. But the story in *Exodus* 3 is certainly open to a variety of interpretations.

What we do know is that Moses while in the wilderness came to the mountain of God, to a place where tradition, at least, suggested that revelation might happen. What is more he came of a race that had already proved that God spoke to men in most unlikely places. An ancestor of his, travelling in a wild bit of country, had taken some stones to make a pillow and settled himself to sleep. In the fading light he had looked across to a hill opposite and seen its rugged shape as a huge stairway cut in rock, and that pattern wove itself into his dreams as "a ladder set up on the earth, and the top of it reached to heaven", and in his dream he heard the voice of God speaking to him. And when he woke he felt "How awesome is this place! This is none other than the house of God, and this is the gate of heaven" (*Genesis* 28. 11–17). It was broad daylight when he said those words, and the place—a wilderness.

Years before another wandering Aramean had been woken from a dream in the middle of the night. Getting up and standing for a moment at the entrance of his tent he had looked up at the starry sky, the kind of sky you can see only in those lands where the air is free of mist, when you feel you can put up your hand and pluck the stars like jewels, they seem so near. And as he looked he heard the voice again, the voice which had started him wandering across the deserts, and knew again that his God, the God who *tells* a man that he is leading him, was in control of the future, however fearful and impossible the present might seem to be (*Genesis* 15. 1-6).

Yes, Moses came of a race that had already been prepared to find God in the wilderness, had, indeed, found him there a veritable shield and an 'exceeding great reward'.

No wonder then that it was back to the same place, to the mountain of God in the wilderness, that Moses came a year or two later, leading this time not a flock of sheep and goats but the people of God to meet with him there in the wilderness. And by that mountain of God there came to that man and his people another revelation of God as a God of holiness who expects his people to be holy, of God as a God of purpose who calls his people to share his purpose, of a God who can lead his people through the wilderness.

That revelation in the wilderness was one of the great turning points of human history. Almost we can say that the Bible is the long-drawn-out drama of man's journey through a wilderness, a drama which more surely than any other points us deep into the mystery of human life and the inner experience of everyman. It is no accident that the greatest allegory of all time, written by a man soaked in the Bible and 'living' in

2

its imagery, begins with the words "As I walk'd through the wilderness of this world".[1]

What is important for us to remember, what the Bible is always insisting, what Bunyan never forgot is that it is the everlasting miracle of the wilderness, of the desert patches of life, that if we are 'listening' and 'looking' we can hear the voice of God and meet him precisely there in the wilderness. Man might have continued to walk with God in a garden. Man chose otherwise. God in his grace meets man in the wilderness of man's own contriving. That is the Gospel. That is why the wilderness is so supremely the place of revelation.

But it is never just a place of revelation. Something happens to the man who has received the revelation, to the people who have heard the voice of God. The man has to become a revealer. He has to 'go, tell'. The people become a people for witness.

And a decisively important part of that witness, central to it, is the assurance that the God who has been heard in the wilderness experience of one people can be discovered in the wilderness experience of all peoples, of everyman. Bunyan spoke truly when he spoke of 'the wilderness of this world'. That was realism not pessimism. Because he saw so clearly the results of sin's erosion in the life of human society he could also paint the picture of the Delectable Mountains and the House Beautiful, and find the valley of humiliation 'a very fruitful place'. He was a prophet of the possibility of reclaiming the wilderness precisely because he was a prophet of the need of the wilderness to be reclaimed.

Go 'tell in the wilderness' is God's command to all who have received his revelation. It is the fundamental

[1] John Bunyan, *Pilgrim's Progress*.

3

term of reference of the Christian Mission, now as always.

Now as always there is urgency in the command. This urgency is forever imprinted on my mind by twenty-four hours of vision once given to me when flying back from Asia to England. I was travelling by flying boat and the last two stops were Basra and Cairo. It was a thrilling experience to land on the two great rivers, the Euphrates and the Nile, which between them enclosed the lands of the Bible. A greater thrill still was to circle slowly round the ruins of Ur of the Chaldees, and then from the observation platform to watch, with my Bible open before me, as that 'plane followed Abraham's route to Haran and then swung south-west across the wilderness he must have travelled till we saw the long line of the mountains of Lebanon and the hill-country of Judaea. And still we flew on over the Dead Sea, over Beersheba, and then along the desert route from Gaza to Egypt, along which an African once 'went on his way rejoicing' having, on that desert road, received the revelation of the Gospel from a man who was obedient to the command, however unexpected and improbable, to 'go tell in the wilderness'. Just before sunset we came down on the Nile after the most exciting piece of Bible study I have ever done.

Next day came the revelation of urgency. In the early morning light we flew up the left arm of the Nile. To the east the land was green, the wonderful green of the delta, for wherever the river came there was life. To the west, stretching to the horizon, was the wilderness. And as I looked down I could see how the desert was encroaching on the town. There were patterns of fields still visible under the coating of sand, there were buried villages, and one could see the waves of sand

4

pressing up against places still inhabited but threatened. Vividly before one's eyes, the panorama of human life was laid bare, the actual life of modern Egypt, the real life of everyman; the glory where the river of life flows freely, death where the desert wins. And yet death is not the last word—in the wilderness lies 'the mountain of God'! Abraham, Jacob, Moses, Amos, Stephen, Philip, Paul, and all the gallant company down the centuries "who through faith conquered kingdoms . . . wandering over deserts" to do so (*Hebrews* 11. 33–38), who all "endured as seeing him who is invisible" (v. 27), then all found God in the wilderness and told of what they had found.

This book is a small part of the 'telling', a record of some of the things learnt in the wilderness in the years of our Lord 1958–59, of things learnt and told. And the key to the telling is to be found in that searching tenth chapter of St. Paul's first letter to the Corinthians, a chapter which most vividly described the wilderness in which the people of the Old Israel once journeyed and the wilderness in which the people of the New Israel still have to travel and bear their witness. Solemnly we are warned of how easily we too may fall in the wilderness. Gloriously we are encouraged because we read that in that same wilderness "they drank from the supernatural rock which followed them, and the rock was Christ". Springs in the desert, pools in the wilderness, the water of life, so the Bible speaks of God's presence. So we are to understand the Christ from whence flow 'rivers of living water'.

"This rock must be published abroad", so Luther expressed it in his great preface to his commentary on the Epistle to the Galatians. What we have to tell in the wilderness is the Gospel of God's mercy in Christ. But we must tell it in great humility. And, because we who tell it are sinners, like those who "were overthrown in the wilderness" (1 *Corinthians* 10. 5), we shall begin by recognizing how difficult we make it for others to hear what we tell because by us the Christ is so often and so easily misrepresented. From there we shall turn to the testimony we have that, nevertheless, the Christ is everywhere and always present. We will show how he makes men free. And yet we shall recognize that in his full glory he is yet to be revealed. This will lead us to consider the context in which we have to reveal him, a context which is part of the 'givenness' of our present situation, something against which we are not to rebel but which we are to accept, praying for

the serenity
To accept the things we cannot change;
The courage to change the things we can,
And the wisdom to know the difference.

With that prayer on our lips we shall consider the principles of our proclamation, the goal of our proclamation, and the methods of our proclamation—in a word, what it means to tell in the wilderness. The epilogue will focus our findings.

The writer is only an amanuensis. He reports what he has heard from some of the men and women who in the wilderness of our world are trying to be obedient to the command, "Go, tell".

O N E

Have I been a wilderness to Israel?

JEREMIAH 2. 31

Can God spread a table in the wilderness?

PSALM 78. 19

They are entangled in the land; the wilderness has shut them in.

EXODUS 14. 3

AMID the babel of voices which bewilder our ears we can, if we listen carefully, distinguish three which should sober us with their reminder that we Christians can by our faithlessness and disobedience make veritable deserts in our own neighbourhoods.

Our three texts represent these three voices. And very commonly, such is our experience, when we have in fact distinguished these three voices from all the rest we hear them speaking at the same time, each addressing us out of the same situation.

The first voice is that of God himself asking how it is that we who have known him should have so completely misunderstood him. It is the same voice which addressed Philip with the words "Have I been with you so long, and yet you do not know me?" (*St. John* 14. 9). God speaks to us out of all our misusings of his grace, our misinterpretations of his Gospel, our misrepresentations of his ways. As we shall see we Christians have created deserts in the name of God.

We are today becoming more and more acutely conscious of these 'Christian-made' deserts and we come

7

very near to despair. Don't we often in our disillusion-
ment, in our consciousness of mistakes made yesterday
whose fruits we gather today, in our awareness of
actions done which can't be undone, of words spoken
beyond recall, hear our own voices tremulous with despair echoing the Psalmist's own echo of an earlier history—"Can God spread a table in the wilderness?"?
Can the years that the locusts have eaten really be
restored? Is there a mountain of God to be discovered
in this wilderness?

And another voice mocks us, the voice of Pharaoh,
the representative of those who do not acknowledge the
Lordship of our Christ—"See these Christians, their
missions and their churches, entangled in the downfall
of the West, shorn of all their privileges, pathetic
minorities, awaiting our victory. See the way they have
taken our caste divisions and our tribal divisions and
multiplied them by their own Church divisions. They
have made their own wilderness and it has shut them
in so that our victory may be the easier".

Yes, we must listen to the voices, listen for our
humbling, yet not without hope. The first voice is the
voice of our God. We have failed him, misunderstood
him, misinterpreted him, misrepresented him, but he
is still our God, even in the wilderness of our own contriving. He makes "the valley of Achor a door of hope"
(*Hosea* 2. 15); the place of unhappy associations (*Joshua*
7. 25–26) will become the place of a new betrothal
(*Hosea* 2. 19).

Bunyan has a word for us as we enter this bit of self-
made wilderness. In Part II of *Pilgrim's Progress* Mr.
Greatheart proposed a riddle to Mr. Honest:

> *He that will kill must first be overcome*
> *Who live abroad would, first must die at-home*

8

Mr. Honest, after some hesitation you remember, gives the right answer:

> *He first by Grace must conquer'd be*
> *That Sin would mortify*
> *And who, that lives, would convince me*
> *Unto himself must die.*

Reading letters which come from all across Tropical Africa from Freetown to Mombasa; from all across the Muslim world from the Temne people of Sierra Leone, through Northern Nigeria and Sudan, across the Middle East to Pakistan and down to Malaya, from India, Pakistan and Ceylon, Singapore, Borneo, Hong Kong and Malaya, right away to Japan; there is a remarkable unanimity of testimony—a disconcerting unanimity of testimony—as to the ways in which Christ is misrepresented.

He is, of course, misrepresented by those who refuse to acknowledge him. But here let us see how we ourselves misrepresent him. I have discovered seven ways of misrepresentation illustrated by these very candid letters. Should the reader of this book live in the British Isles or North America, in Western Europe or Australia or New Zealand or South Africa let him ask himself whether he seriously imagines that he can reduce this number, even by one, as regards the little bit of wilderness he knows.

The *first* of the 'seven deadly misrepresentations' is the confusion we have created between the Gospel and our western way of life, between our message and the colour of our skins, between our 'nationalisms' and the universal Christ, and because by our failures we have passed these misrepresentations on to the Church in Asia and Africa. Caste still riddles the Church in India, tribalism still disfigures the Church in Africa. We seem to have no message for a world of competing nationalisms and mounting racialism.

We of the West cannot separate ourselves from our fellow-countrymen or from our history, nor ought we to wish to do so. One of our missionaries in Uganda was warned by a much respected English political officer against inviting Africans to share in the monthly celebration of Holy Communion in English at the mission church. "If you do that, Padre," he said, "you'll never get your Europeans coming along. They'll not stand for it." As the missionary remarked: "His tone of voice was such as to say that he would be the first who would not stand for it."

In an adjacent African territory another missionary heard one European say, on seeing an African in church: "What's that confounded wog doing in here?" To the same missionary other European Anglican churchgoers said about their fellow-Anglicans who happened to be Africans: "They're an inferior race, old man."

So still in 1959 the same pathetic tale goes on across the world. But we dare not 'withdraw our skirts' from these white Anglicans abroad who make nonsense of the Faith. They came out to Africa from parish churches in England. Had they ever heard from their pulpits any guidance whatever about their Christian duty as Anglicans to their fellow-Anglicans of another race? Had they been taught in their confirmation classes about their duty to their neighbour, and had that linked up with the Samaritan who looked after a Jew; and then been told that Confirmation, amongst other things, was designed to give them the grace to "go and do likewise" in their own neighbourhood, and possibly in Africa? Sometimes perhaps. All too often, no!

We can thank God for the many in government service and in business life, and others who are living and working in Africa and Asia, who are aliens in those lands, and who yet live as members of the commonwealth of God. But unfortunately one mis-representation is far more obvious and is much more noticeable than the faithful representation of those who quietly day by day acknowledge Christ in the presence of their fellows irrespective of colour or race.

The one fundamental question in East, Central and South Africa today is the question: "Are we going to treat the African with genuine respect for his personal worth as a human being?" He has not received much treatment of this kind yet. Time is running out.

But do not let any of us in the missionary movement think we can contract out of this tragedy of misrepre-sentation. Very few of us are in a position to take up a 'holier-than-thou' attitude on the subject of race pre-judice. There is a place for most of us at the penitent bench.

Meanwhile there are so many ways in which un-willingly, perhaps inevitably, we add to the confusion. Christianity is identified with the culture of the West and its national policies. The very 'foreignness' of the missionary is always a potential liability (even when it is from another point of view an asset) until the local Church is obviously not dependent on the missionary. That point occurs in a letter from Iran.

In the opposite sense a missionary from the Upper Nile can write of the danger of so 'nationalizing' the local Church as to run the risk of obscuring the essen-tially international character of the Church. He says pertinently enough: "In being supersensitive to our racial and 'foreign' position within the Church in a developing nationalistic situation, both we and the local Church are apt to lose sight of the real significance of our presence, as the witness to, and surety of, the local Church's supra-nationalism."

A subtle point comes in a letter from Sudan: "We missionaries tend to live in 'ivory castles' and, therefore, the message that we preach appears to be relevant only at a circumscribed area of the lives of the people. We live English lives here in Africa and the result is that the Gospel is communicated by us to Africans only at those few points where our lives really touch theirs; in the classroom and in the church building."

An Australian missionary sends this comment from India speaking of the Indian reaction to the 'White Australia' policy. "We cannot escape our citizenship—we cannot disown our country. And our witness and friendship as representatives of the Australian Church are marred by this corporate sin, which we, as Australians, carry—acquiescence, by apathetic inaction, in a national policy which, whatever the motive behind it, appears as a direct negation of the Gospel which we preach."

No, "we cannot escape our citizenship". We have to go through the wilderness.

The *second* 'deadly misrepresentation' is that of Christian disunity, and that of two kinds, disunity between different Christian Churches, and disunity within the same Church, and in both cases a failure to 'discern the Lord's Body'.

It is a humiliating fact that the Communist Government of China has recently encouraged the Christians of China to denounce their denominational differences as being the legacy of 'foreign missionary imperialism'. That, alas, is not a denunciation which can be laughed off, as any student of missionary history knows all too well. And still, despite the great 'leap forward' made in South India, despite the plans for Church union in Ceylon and North India, despite the explorations towards Church unity in West Africa, and the tortoise-like progress in the Provinces of Canterbury and York, deep suspicions continue to separate even those Churches which meet to discuss their common problems under the auspices of the World Council of Churches, and of National Councils of Churches. The 'inside' story of all too many union institutions makes melancholy reading.

Yet some slight progress is being made here and there by those Churches which are part of the Ecumenical Movement. What is most serious, and what comes back as the testimony of almost every area where our missionaries are at work, is the hardening of the lines of division between the three groups of Christians, those in the Ecumenical Movement, those of the Roman obedience, and those of the Pentecostal and associated Churches.

Here are three out of many illustrations. The first, a poignantly personal one, comes from Japan. "Miriam came to see me," writes a missionary, "and said 'My father, who was a drunkard, has been converted and joined the Pentecostal Church to which my sister and mother go. They tell me that because I am an Anglican our Christian witness is divided and that it is this that is preventing the other members of the family from coming to Christ. What ought I to do?' 'What do you think yourself?' I asked, 'I can worship better in the Anglican Church, but I feel that I should go to the Pentecostal Church, if that would save the others. Christ is not divided and I think that he will accept my sacrifice and help my family into true faith in him'."

A second illustration comes from the north of India. "A C.I.D. Inspector who had been appointed to find out about missionary activity in this area, especially among the Roman Catholics, came to our veranda for help in understanding the difference between Roman Catholics and Protestants. He put it in this way, 'What is the difference between your Christ and their Christ?'"

A third illustration comes from Nigeria. A missionary writes: "The really shameful divisions are the water-tight ones which separate Roman Catholic, Protestant and Pentecostalist. There is incontrovertible evidence from many different parts of the diocese that many of the methods used by the Roman Catholics in seeking to win proselytes are not those we can regard as Chris-tian. Many who wish to understand this challenge and to meet it with love are baffled and shocked, and so are frustrated in their attempts to help the Church to meet the 'Roman Catholic challenge' in the right spirit." There is a *cri de coeur* concealed in that quotation which finds its echo from every single area in Africa where we are working. The invitation to an ecumenical con-ference recently sent out by the newly-elected Pope is a welcome move in the right direction. May we soon see some evidence of the impact of this invitation at the grass-roots policies of the Roman Church in Africa. Meanwhile a purely negative attitude by ourselves is quite inadequate. The major scandal of a divided Christianity calls for every effort to begin building the bridge from our side of the gulf. Else we condone the misrepresentation of the Christ.

Meanwhile having brought our divisions from Europe we have found plenty of imitators in Africa. One Nigerian village boasts three Churches whose vary-ing titles are "The Church of Christ"; "The True Church of Christ"; and "The only True Church of Christ".

But if divisions *between* Churches are tragic scarcely less so are the divisions within the Churches. Let one illustration from India stand for all the others that might be quoted. "While travelling by bus one day in India," writes a missionary, "I found myself sitting next to a young man who had been a patient in the hospital where I work. He told me he had bought a New Testament, after attending hospital services, and talking with the nurses. He said 'I have been reading this, and I am very interested, especially in the life Jesus lived, and the way of life that he taught. I know many of the Christians round here, and what I cannot understand is why you live so differently from what you preach. There is so much quarrelling among you, one family with another, and rivalry and jealousy in your churches, between one parish and another. You preach what it says in this book that you love one another and that you are all one in Christ Jesus. Why do you live so differently from this?'."

The missionary continues in her letter: "This man, like many others, was drawn to Christ by what he had heard and read. Watching us Christians he found some of us fighting over land, one parish jealous of another, because more was being done by missionaries in one than the other; family quarrels over marriage arrangements; Christian leaders failing to agree. He and others like him go away disappointed, or disgusted, or disillusioned, because they see only a Christ misrepresented by our disunity."

Are those Indian parishes unique? Could it happen anywhere else? Everything O.K. with you? Then praise the Lord and read 1 *Corinthians* 10 *very* slowly, pausing for prayer at verse 12.

The *third* 'deadly misrepresentation' is the widespread prevalence of legalism, of a pharisaic attitude to those who have sinned, and a common misuse of the sacraments as having been primarily designed as a means of discipline rather than a means of grace.

An Australian missionary writing from Tanganyika gives an illustration which may stand for other parts of the world and which, in the questions it raises, poses a whole range of missionary problems. He writes: "One of the first things that struck me as strange in the life of the Church in Tanganyika was the Council of Elders in each parish who sit and 'hear shauris'. One can almost say 'who sit in judgment on their fellow-sinners'. Even now after nine years I am still uncomfortable in these 'cases'. Whether it is a particularly 'mission field' way of exercising a pastoral ministry or a particularly 'African' way I do not know. That it has stood a certain test of time I do not doubt. Attempts to transform it from within are disturbing—to do away with it would be to do away with the security it affords many people.

"Many folk think of suspension from Communion as a punishment rather than an incentive to repentance. It has even been heard that a man in front of such a council has pleaded 'Give me my punishment and let me go'. And Elders of the Church say 'I was given six months—of course this man must be given six months'. The Church in Action has travelled a long way from him who asked 'Who made me a judge and a divider among you?'"

Somewhere along the line our teaching has gone sadly awry. Is it perhaps that we have stressed too much the way of salvation as being an individual adventure, and so have had to call in a legal system to deal with individual aberrations? Have we stressed enough the idea of the community of Christians as the society of the divine forgiveness? Those queries come in a letter from South India.

The *fourth* 'deadly misrepresentation' would also seem to have been introduced from abroad. A number of writers refer to the appalling 'dullness' of Christian worship, and an even commoner report is of the essentially negative attitude to life assumed to go with being a truly converted Christian. "Touch not, taste not, handle not"—life by rule, a negative rule at that, is a very natural stage in the spiritual life. It offers the framework of a self-discipline that may be of real value to the individual. Where it becomes a new bondage is when it is treated as of universal application. Paul was all for self-discipline. Did he not say "I pommel my body and subdue it, lest after preaching to others I myself should be disqualified" (1 *Corinthians* 9. 27)? Yet he never allowed his own self-discipline to become a rule binding others. His view was made very clear in *Colossians* 2 where, speaking of regulations framed to fit everyone, he says "These have an appearance of wisdom in promoting rigor of devotion and self-abasement and severity to the body, but they are of no value in checking the indulgence of the flesh" (v. 23).

The trouble with 'working to rule' in all its forms is that it destroys the liberty of the Spirit, and very easily, in worship, becomes a pedantic slavery to the letter at the expense of living experience.

In this way, often with the very best of intentions and sometimes with a most conscientious loyalty to what is believed to be 'the pattern set on the mount' Christ is misrepresented. When as happens in some places English hymns are translated into a highly tonal language and then the translation is sung to the traditional English tune the result is 'sacred gibberish' and surely comes under the condemnation of 1 *Corinthians* 14. 9.

Again and again during our visit to West Africa in 1957 my wife and I joined in worship in Nigerian churches and what joyful occasions these were. But what struck us again and again was the contrast in the singing and the 'life' of this service when, for instance, a well-known hymn had been sung to an English tune and then we had a hymn set to an African chant. The first was dutiful, carefully rendered, reverent. The second was ecstatic with spontaneous overflow of the heart praising God in its own idiom.

Changes are on the way, changes in the right direction, but the pace of change is slow and meanwhile the joy of Christ is misrepresented.

The *fifth* 'deadly misrepresentation' can best be introduced by drawing attention to the fact that after we had painstakingly provided our own patterns of parliamentary procedure to the peoples over whom we ruled, they have, one by one, after trying them out under the conditions of their own political independence, jettisoned them as not being according to their own genius. Have we any reason for believing that our British ecclesiastical machinery will be maintained once we genuinely take our hands off the steering? That is a very unpopular question but it needs to be pressed home. It cannot be answered yet but it will be a valuable exercise for us foreigners to have a little healthy scepticism, if not a suspended judgment, about the universal validity of our own methods of organization.

To illustrate this I quote from a very interesting letter from one of our missionaries, a man who has carried great responsibility in the diocese in which he serves and has gladly relinquished it to Indian hands. Commenting on the contrast between the Church of the first century A.D. and the Church in India today he writes: "And now, in contrast to the first century, it is the Mother Church which helps and supports the daughter Churches and gives them, in the end, a ready-made written constitution which cannot grow but, if anything, only decays. We see the same kind of imposition in matters of prayer book revision, where the Church concerned accepts a ready-made form of worship which, by the very perfection of its form and arrangement, enslaves the infant Church at the very beginning and virtually prevents it from developing its own forms. It seems to me that this is the fundamental way in which Christ is misrepresented by the 'sending' Churches today. We dominate the situation. And it doesn't necessarily help that we sleep on a mud floor and eat off a brass plate and go all Indian or all African."

The *sixth* 'deadly misrepresentation' is inconsistent living. I quote from a letter from India which, with slightly different local colouring, might so easily have come from any one of the dioceses of the Anglican Communion. It is altogether too typical to be comfortable as an illustration of the false separation of the secular and the sacred. "There is a Christian family living just behind us. . . . At one moment our house is penetrated with the noise of screaming, beating, abusive language and yet the next moment we hear them singing very well indeed the most sacred and beautiful hymns. Have we somehow so misrepresented Christ that absolutely no relationship can be seen between worshipping him and our daily lives . . .? In a vast Christian community of this kind one finds that for the majority Christianity has absolutely nothing to do with the way they behave in their relationship with others."

Have we got the mirror tilted so that we are looking straight into it ourselves?

The *seventh* 'deadly misrepresentation' is our own personal failure to be 'Christ' to other men and women.

Let one missionary speak for all missionaries, but not only for missionaries, for the writer of this book also and for all its readers. "In thinking over many things this furlough," the missionary writes, "it has struck me in how many ways I have not been 'poor in spirit', not readily available, not a 'giving' person. Whether we live in big mission houses, or institutions, or more simply among the people, in so far as we have not shared 'ourselves' in friendship and hospitality, in openness as fellow-sinners, in our weakness as well as in the richness of our own inheritance, we have mis-represented Christ."

As we have considered each one of these 'deadly misrepresentations' have we been listening to those three voices—the questioning voice of Christ, the querulous voice of our own despair, the mocking voice of Pharaoh? They have been speaking all the time whether we heard them or not. Those three voices must not be 'faded out'. All three must be listened to and their measure taken before we can hope to tell in the wilderness the wonderful works of God.

T W O

"Lo, I am with you always, to the close of the age"
—with those words St. Matthew ends his Gospel,
leaving us *with* Jesus our Lord as we go out in obedience
to his command to make disciples of all nations. "I am
with you always" is an echo of the revelation at the
burning bush at the foot of the mountain of God.

Some understanding of what happened to Moses in
the wilderness will prepare us to enter more fully into
the meaning of the ever-present Christ. At the burning
bush Moses discovered three truths about God, truths
which can transfigure any wilderness.

First God reveals himself as unchanging in the deepest
sense of reliable. "I am the God of your father"
(*Exodus* 3. 6). The revelation begins intimately. Moses
is linked directly with the father he never knew by the
link of the living God. Only then does God reveal himself as no local spirit on a haunted mountain but as
the God of history; the "God of Abraham, the God of
Isaac, the God of Jacob". The God who made
Abraham a wanderer trusting a promise he would not
see fulfilled was the same God who stopped Isaac from
wandering and told him to settle down (*Genesis* 26. 3),
and who at the ford Jabbok gave to Jacob a new name
as a symbol of redemption (*Genesis* 32. 28)—the God of
one unchanging redemptive purpose, working now
after one fashion, now after another, but always at

work, and now about to work again most strangely through Moses. That was the first discovery at the burning bush in the wilderness.

The *second* discovery was an assurance about the future—"I will be with you" (*Exodus* 3. 12). This whole dialogue between God and Moses is full of promises about the future. It is as though in answer to Moses' question "By what name shall I call you?" God says "I am the abiding presence". Yet there is even more than this that was made clear to Moses as the bush burned and was not consumed. The word 'I am' is no philosophic abstraction, a declaration of the 'Being' of God. Rather it is essentially a dynamic word indicating happening, becoming, all that we mean by presence, a living presence which is both known and incalculable. God is a God who will always be present but present "in many and various ways" (*Hebrews* 1. 1). The God who will be present with Moses is a God who is always a free agent. The initiative is always with God.

We shall best understand the *third* discovery Moses made if we remember his background. The adopted son of Pharaoh's daughter, brought up in a palace, he was "instructed in all the wisdom of the Egyptians" (*Acts* 7. 22). In that ancient Egypt "religion was in practice little more than regulated magic" (*Buber*). If you knew the right formula you could control the actions of your god. Moses had to be disinfected of that false idea of religion if he was ever to enter into the mystery of the God who is always present, present not to be commanded but to command. "My presence does not need to be conjured up. Lo, I am with you always." Moses went out from that revelation "the servant of the Lord".

In such threefold guise we are to understand the

promise of God at a later critical moment in the wilderness journey when he said to Moses "My presence will go with you, and I will give you rest" (*Exodus* 33. 14). That promise renewed by Jesus, our Lord, is valid still in every wilderness, and not least in that Christian-contrived wilderness we studied in the last chapter. The servant of God may tragically have misrepresented his Master. But the Master remains utterly reliable. His purpose of love, of redemption, does not change. Furthermore the initiative always remains with him. We do not anticipate him. He meets us at the place appointed. His continuing presence at all times and in every place is not to be commanded but to be recognized, welcomed and obeyed.

That is the abiding inspiration of the missionary task, the assurance that though we be faithless he remains faithful (2 *Timothy* 2. 13), faithful to his purpose, faithful to his promises, faithful to those to whom we go and tell about him, faithful to us who tell.

In 'many and various ways' this faithfulness of God is revealed.

A missionary from Iran tells this story of the divine initiative, of the presence of God anticipating the presence of his messengers, of a God who is still to be found in the wilderness. In a Persian village there was a woman who knew nothing of Christ but had vaguely heard of people called Christians. In a dream she had a vision of Christ who came to her and led her by the hand. Waking from her dream she came into Isfahan to try to find him. It was as simple and direct as that. Enquiries about Christ led her to be directed to the Christian hospital. There she asked to be shown a picture of Christ so that she might be sure that it was the same person she had seen in her dreams. Fortunately the missionaries were wise and did not show her any picture at all but read to her from the Gospels. *There* she met him—a remarkable vindication incidentally of the reality of her dream and of the reality of the Gospel story. She was baptized and has been a faithful witnessing Christian ever since, undeterred by persecution.

From East Africa comes the story of another Muslim, this time a man, who also had a dream. In his dream he saw Christ standing on the steps of the Temple in Jerusalem calling to him. He responded to that dream first by carefully reading side by side the Bible and the Qur'an. Then he decided to accept Christ and "is now counting the cost of baptism".

Both these stories are illustrative in more ways than one. Both speak of the self-authenticating message of the Bible. One points to the Christ-authenticating witness of a Christian hospital, and by inference of the Christian doctors and nurses in that hospital. Behind that Persian Bible and that Swahili Bible is the Bible Society. In both—in spite of all its failures and misrepresentations—is the Church of Christ, the Church of the ages, transmitting the Scriptures, bearing the apostolic testimony, telling of the God whose love does not change.

But I see something more. I see the Christ present in the world of Islam. Those two stories were stories of dreams. Dreams tell us of the world below the level of our consciousness, the world upon which unrecognized impressions are continually being made without our realizing at all what is happening. Someone has even defined grace as "the great God himself permeating our subconscious". Now deep below the surface consciousness of Muslims there is the permeating influence of the Qur'an. And the Qur'an bears eloquent testimony to Jesus. We may well claim that it is inadequate testimony, we may point to where it is

24

gravely inaccurate, but testimony there is, and not least to his second coming. Jesus is indeed a mystery in Islam. Islam cannot get away from Jesus. A Muslim by the strictest canons of orthodoxy must expect Jesus to come. Here, surely, is a preparation which we may not be able to use with great effect for the Gospel, but which Jesus can use. It would appear quite certain that in his own gracious and gentle way he is using it. He is not to be conjured up but he is always present, yes, in Islam also. In those two stories above a man and a woman recognized him.

Can we have any serious doubt that, although after a different fashion, the ever-present Christ is at work within the world of Hinduism?

From darkness lead us to light
and from shadows to reality

That is a prayer that goes back to the earliest sources of Hinduism. It is a cry into the night addressed to no known god. Of India perhaps more surely than anywhere else it is legitimate to speak of man's search for the unknown God.

"One day," writes a missionary from North India, "I had to visit the Income Tax Officer who had recently come to take up his post in the town. After we had conducted our business, he showed me a paper setting out the very high ideals of devotion, prayer, discipline and service of his particular sect of Hinduism, by which he tried to live. I was struck by the tremendous desire of such a man for God who was to be sought after at great cost. He knew nothing of the free gift of grace, and probably he would never accept it, yet the *desire* was there."

The *desire* was there. Can we doubt that the Desire

of all nations was also there in that Income Tax Office? He was there in that Hindu man's desire. He was there in the person of that Christian. He was there in their attempt at mutual understanding. So it is everywhere in India where Christian and non-Christian meet in genuine respect for each other, wherever love is allowed to work its miracles, be the process never so gradual yet it is sure.

> *I come in the little things,*
> *Saith the Lord:*
> *My starry wings*
> *I do forsake,*
> *Love's highway of humility to take:*
> *Meekly I fit My stature to your need.*
> *In beggar's part*
> *About your gates I shall not cease to plead—*
> *As man, to speak with man—*
> *Till by such art*
> *I shall achieve My Immemorial Plan,*
> *Pass the low lintel of the human heart.*[1]

Despite all the misrepresentations of our Lord which have accompanied the telling of the good news about God in the wilderness of India's life, innumerable holy and humble men and women have in fact lived and worked and died there for Christ's sake and India's. The besieging of India by love may be long-drawn-out but the end is sure. Christ has found his way into the heart of India. His presence, infinitely winsome, infinitely exasperating, is there. The immensely increased sense of urgency in India's quest of the unknown God, which has become more and more apparent in the last hundred years, is the direct result of the modern mis-

[1] From the poem "Immanence", by Evelyn Underhill, *Oxford Book of English Mystical Verse* (O.U.P., 1942), p. 525.

sionary movement of the Christian Church. When the last word has been said about the 'awfulness' of foreign missionaries, and an awful lot can be said, let us remember that the last word is with God.

> *This is His will: He takes and*
> > *He refuses,*
> *Finds Him ambassadors whom men deny,*
> *Wise ones nor mighty for His saints*
> > *He chooses,*
> *No, such as John or Gideon or I*[1]

Here is another illustration of the improbable and the unexpected as showing the impact of the Christ upon the imagination of India. I have before me as I write a leaflet advertising a play entitled *The Life of Jesus Christ*. Once a year a Hindu company of Tamil actors puts on this play. It is in fifty-two scenes, runs for four hours and is watched by four thousand people at a time, the overwhelming majority of them Hindus. One who saw the play said that it was performed with 'very great reverence'.

No, there is no knowing when, where or in what form the Presence will be revealed. What is asked of us who serve the Presence is, above all, expectancy. "I had been invited to take part in a refresher course for university lecturers in English," writes a missionary. "At the end of a strenuous morning and afternoon at lecturing, discussion groups and demonstration lessons, I took a grass mat and lay out to rest under the trees. After a few minutes—far too few for me—one member of the course spread out a mat alongside mine. I steeled myself for more probing on teaching techniques and academic questions. However, the first question took

[1] From "St. Paul", by F. W. H. Myers.

us off on a surprisingly new tack. The question came abruptly out of the heavy, sleepy heat: 'What part does your belief in God play in this job you are doing?' The questioner was not a Christian. Then a little later along the line: 'Faith in Jesus Christ may be a necessary part of *your* religion, but why should that be necessary for an Indian?' And so, until mosquitoes and red ants drove us indoors in the hot dusk, we explored together the initial steps of my companion's response to God's call to him. Nothing was further from my intentions that hot, weary evening. The initiative was God's."

Few things are more exciting on the wilderness trail than to discover the way God has already gone ahead of you. An illustration comes to hand, again from India.

A nursing sister writes: "Last year we broke new ground when from the hospital we started a village health service. This was something quite new to the people and we wondered how it would work, would we be welcome, would there be any opportunities at all to help? We need not have worried. It was just as if Christ had prepared it all and was waiting for us. We received friendship and help from many homes. In one village there was already a village council sponsored by government, with a programme for making various improvements in the village. The leader welcomed us, was most interested in our plans for health teaching, and took on the task of distributing milk to the school-children and others in the homes when needed. In another village we found the high-caste landowner very welcoming and interested. He organized meetings for us so that we could give health talks, helped us about visiting sick folk, and also took on the distribution of the milk.

"In this tiny corner of the world were people to

whom any idea of preventing disease was unheard of, and completely alien to their thinking, and yet when we felt called to start this aspect of Christian healing among them, there were just one or two minds already prepared to understand and help."

She ends with these words "Christ is present and working in every place to which he calls us".

And he is no less surely present, as he promised, where two or three are gathered together in his Name. We very easily assume, and quite wrongly, that the promise is primarily related to meetings for prayer. But we do not meet in his Name only to pray. Every occasion and activity when Christians meet should be 'in his Name'. The letters which have come to me in connection with this book are full of illustrations of how vividly the presence of Christ was realized by Christians doing things together—a hospital in one place with an African nursing sister bringing to a nervous European patient the reassuring 'presence' of Christ: an art class working together on a difficult task involving sustained attention over a long period, and calling for not a little disciplined drudgery and the Christ very real in the midst: a women's training centre of which a missionary could say "in every situation which arises out of our living together Christ is met in someone involved".

"Always present"—the 'continuing present' of the grammar book has to find its equivalent in experience if there is to be a valid testimony. That is the emphasis of the Revival Movement in East Africa which has a disconcerting habit of expecting Christians to take seriously the words "New every morning is the love" and to have something new to say about it every morning! That is an insight which all our Christianity badly needs.

Incidentally it suggests a dynamic approach to the study of theology! A staff member of an overseas theological college writes: "I may come into the classroom to teach Doctrine. I may speak of the Cross, or of the history of the Church's teaching of the Cross. I may illustrate by saying how the Cross first became a living reality to me. But one more step remains. My students and brothers must know that they and I are experiencing still *today* the forgiveness and the power of the Cross. And even that, we shall understand, is only 'salvation *so far*'." Theology becoming contemporary! How infinitely exciting, and how indisputably true to the New Testament, as anyone will discover who studies the tenses used by Paul when he speaks of salvation.

What is more, a genuinely contemporary theology—a theology of the always present Christ who cannot be 'conjured up'—will do something to save earnest Christians from the very common mistake of thinking that the Lord Christ is only 'present' when the right words are used. That idea really belongs to the religion of magic. Martin Buber was surely right when he insisted that "in the revelation at the Burning Bush religion is demagicized".

Christ is always present. On that truth as our daily ration we can travel through any wilderness. And some of his people he now leads through the wilderness of pain. Because some who will read these words may do so while travelling through that wilderness let me close this chapter by quoting from a letter from Japan about a woman who turned her wilderness into a well of water for others. She was a kindergarten teacher. As a result of the war she developed spinal tuberculosis and was on her bed for more than six years. One of our missionaries writes: "Her only complaint was that she could not be working for God. I told her that her prayers could be a greater work than those of us who were rushing around. Every time I visited her I came away challenged and strengthened, and felt I had met Christ there. She was, and still is, completely selfless, following very closely in her Master's footsteps so that many, young and old, go to her for advice and comfort. Her doctor saw Christ in her and became a Christian with all his family."

T H R E E

He found him in a desert land, and in the howling waste of the wilderness; he encircled him, he cared for him, and he kept him as the apple of his eye. DEUTERONOMY 32. 10

WHAT a vivid picture! We see the man first of all in his aloneness. There is no one else in sight. The desert stretches lifeless to the horizon whichever way you look. The man is lost. There may be tracks in the desert but he does not know how to read the signs. He is very much alone, except for the fears that keep him company. Suddenly in that howling waste he sees a distant figure moving rapidly towards him. The stranger knows the way. He is no longer isolated, alone and afraid. He has been found. He is taken to the neighbouring encampment, made to feel at-home, encircled, cared for.

The New Testament parallel is the story of the Prodigal Son, who was lost and was found. But our text points beyond the individual. For the wanderer was in fact the wandering people of Israel personified by the poet. In his poem he shows us God going out into the wilderness to find his own. And at once we recognize another link with the New Testament, with the story of the Lost Sheep.

Perhaps we can begin to see what all this means for our lost humanity if deliberately we turn our backs for a moment upon the howling waste of our terror-haunted civilization and see what the Gospel can do for a simpler people who yet are all their lifetime in bondage to fear. Let us follow two of our missionaries, a doctor and an agriculturist, as with an African padre they move about among the Giryama people in the coastal province of Kenya.

Here is a primitive pagan people hardly touched by the rapid changes elsewhere in Kenya. They are still practising the age-old 'shifting cultivation' whereby, having exhausted the fertility of one patch of sandy soil, they move on, clear a bit more of the forest in which to plant maize or millet, and so the cycle goes on. Their faith is that of other primitive peoples, a close linking of the seen with the unseen, of this material world with the world of spirits. Upon a right relation between the two worlds, prosperity, health, life itself depends. Easily such a faith turns to a morbid concern to make sure that the unseen world of spirits, suspected of being malevolent, shall be appeased. The medium of appeasement, a medium in more senses than one, is the spirit-doctor, whose witchcraft is the art of dealing with the unseen and the unknown. Let our agriculturist missionary take up the tale.

"Come with me to Petero's village. He is one of many Christians who has 'gone back'. When we arrived we found him out, we chatted with his wife and invited her to a meeting at the church, but as we were about to leave she told us about Bendera. We were led to a very small windowless hut and in the gloom saw a thin small figure sitting hunched over smouldering embers. She was obviously ill, thin and frail, and we strongly advised the family to bring her to see the doctor at the hospital. We talked to her and then called the family together to pray. We knelt on the dusty floor and in the smoky atmosphere prayed to the Great Physician for her healing.

"We left after that but I could not forget Bendera, and as she was not brought to the doctor, I asked the doctor and the padre to come to see her. The doctor was in process of examining her when we realized that this was not organic illness but 'demon' possession. She was shaking all over, her head tossing back and forth, shouting, groaning, and although still sitting she seemed unconscious. We were not alone now. Her husband, brothers and sisters, Petero and her old mother were there, and also a stranger who sat silently and almost motionless in the corner of the hut. She was wearing beads and special bracelets. She had been called in to help. She was a medicine woman and although once baptized was now, to use her own words, 'serving Satan'.

"Here was a village in bondage. And this was where our evangelism had to begin. We had to go to Petero and his family and make known the Saviour who can make men free."

He can and he does.

The letter goes on: "A few days later we arrived at another village, and were greeted by a crowd of cheerful expectant Christians. 'Praise the Lord,' they said, and they meant it. Here were men and women truly set free in a land of darkness and bondage."

With that village as a base other villages were visited. "Almost the first one we came to had a witness to him who sets men free. A middle-aged woman came out to greet us. She wore the typical dress of a pagan Giryama woman but with a difference. She had no charms adorning her neck, wrists or ankles. Instead she had a wonderful smile. 'This woman has been saved,' the padre told me. 'She couldn't read, and up till a few weeks ago she had never been to church.' I asked how it happened. 'It was through her old mother,' he replied. 'She was ill and in great need and then she heard the testimony of one who had been set free by Jesus, and there and then she burned up all her charms and trusted the Lord. When this woman saw the difference in her old mother she started coming to church to hear the word of God and now she has been saved.'"

There is a New Testament touch in that story, don't you think?

From another part of Africa, Southern Sudan, comes the record of freedom not just from fear of the spirits, but from fear of death.

"He was a friend of many years whose warm handshake and smile were always a joy. His was a quiet steadfast faith always. He bore the test of the breakdown of his wife's health and reason without murmuring against God or seeking another marriage, though pressure was put upon him. His health was never very robust yet it came as a great shock to all his friends when he had a sudden haemorrhage and was taken off to hospital where he died soon after. Those who saw him there were all amazed at his quietness and peace. 'Tell them not to trouble,' he said to a friend, as hospital attendants tried to fix up a blood transfusion. 'The Lord has called me and I am going to him.' Though his wife and children were ninety miles away and there was no time to make arrangements for them he did not fret but quietly committed them to his friends. He looked at death and was unafraid because for him it was the gateway to the Lord whom he loved and had followed steadfastly for so many years."

From Uganda comes further evidence of this Christian freedom from fears of all kinds which in turn have changed the very attitude to death. A letter contains the following incidents.

"I think now of two particular funerals I have attended. One was miles off in the bush, in the coffee garden of a home where for some years, contrary to local custom, a widowed mother-in-law had lived in her daughter-in-law's home. And had lived at peace, contrary to local beliefs, for the custom is intended only to preserve the peace!

"At the grave her will was read, a joyful glad testimony to her Saviour, and saying how only Jesus could have done what they saw happening now, bringing home to himself one who had lived peacefully and joyfully with her daughter-in-law. And then the daughter-in-law spoke, testifying to the power of the Lord to help them to repent whenever there had been occasion. Punctuating this unusual scene came the joyful singing of the brethren gathered round the graveside. Many of them gave glad witness also to the power of the same Lord. What struck me was not so much that here was an answer to fears of death, but that for these Christians *death did not exist*. The presence of Jesus *means* just that.

"It was just the same about a year later when I attended the funeral of a little girl, the daughter of one of my greatest friends. He was a member of staff. Students had dug the grave. Students carried the little bundle to it. We prayed. Then Absalom spoke, quite simply, saying how the Lord was their joy in this time, and how he had done that good thing for which they were praising him. His wife added her own words too, and they sang with us all.

"So it is not just at times when the old are taken. Christ *has* the keys of death, and shares his joys in all those times."

We are already a long way away from the smoke-filled hut in the Giryama country and well on our way back to what we call civilization. How many funerals can you remember attending in England with something comparable to the spirit of that funeral in the African bush? I can remember only a few. But yet there are Europeans, professing Christians, who will blandly tell you that these Africans are "an inferior people, old man".

When you tread the verge of Jordan don't you hope you'll have a faith like one of those African Christians? I do. Two great friends of mine, missionaries, had just such a faith as had Absalom and his wife, when they buried their little daughter. And a bystander marvelling was won for Christ. I wonder how I would have faced it. What about you? It isn't only in Africa that Christ can deal with fear, and with death.

Let us leave these particular fears with one more story, and leave them with a twinkle in our eyes also. This is a simple story of another man of Sudan who had been set free by Christ from fear of witchcraft. Look out for the twinkle—and don't under-estimate just how miraculous, properly miraculous, a twinkle can be.

"One of our men had a spell put on him by a relative of the local Rainmaker—a most unhealthy thing to happen. It was not just a spell to sickness but to death. The 'victim' was present when I was told about it by some of the other men. He was obviously quite untroubled. 'If the Lord wants me he will take me, it may be next week and that would please Asengaja (*the caster of the spell*) greatly; it may be next year, or in twenty years' time. It may even be (*with a twinkle in his eye*) that Asengaja will be called first.' Through the weeks that have followed he has remained quite unperturbed by a happening which for many would have been an unbearable burden."

I have put freedom from fear and freedom in the presence of death, first of all because these do in fact for the vast majority of mankind appear as a far greater bondage than sin. Here I give only one very simple illustration of Christ's power to set men free from sin. It is so simple that any one of us can easily imagine ourselves into the same place, and by the grace of God, if we should in fact find ourselves there, into the same release. Here is the Christ in action.

"I was about to leave for furlough," writes the member of a theological college staff. "In the busy rushing around college of the last few days, a student stopped me. He had a library book in his hand, and was not quick to get to the point. I wondered what was coming, for in his class this was one who had obviously had something on his mind, something holding him back, for months past.

"'Before you go,' he began, 'there's something I want to put right with you as the Librarian. About six months ago I took a book from the library, and in it I found some stamps. At the time I used them, intending to replace them later. This I have never done, despite knowing from time to time that this was on my conscience. Please advise me now, while I still have the chance to put it right.'

"A small thing, easily set right. There were others involving a journey of many miles about a debt the man concerned had never noticed. Yet these things had been setting the lad back in his Christian life so much that it was noticed in his class work.

"It is in the working through of repentance, and in taking seriously Christ's warning 'If thou remember . . . go first', that he is teaching his people release from guilt and fears such as that student's."

Do we smile indulgently? Even perhaps murmur

something about 'scrupulosity', and the danger of getting morbid? Let us remember that it is "the little foxes, that spoil the vineyards" (*Song of Solomon* 2.15). Is there any country where integrity is not at a premium today, integrity at every level and in every relationship, in every occupation?

In the loneliness of sin Christ can find us, en-circle us in the fellowship of grace, care for us, keep us—that is the Gospel we have to tell in the wilderness to everyone we find there. A major part of the missionary enterprise is doing just that. After all, he was called Jesus "for he will save his people from their sins" (*St. Matthew* 1.21).

There are other freedoms which the Gospel offers men and which are there in the wilderness for the telling. One teller puts it like this : "When one student came to us, deep down she was unhappy, full of fears and anxieties, and always seemed to look on the dark side of life. She had understood nothing of the joy of the Resurrection. At the beginning of the course she had to fight a real battle against resentment, for she found it difficult to accept the routine life of discipline and concentrated study which was expected of her; to her it seemed that this should only be expected of paid workers, not voluntary!"

A thoroughly negative attitude to life—haven't we all met it, perhaps even shared it? Two Christian women, one Indian and one English, shared their home with this student and slowly but surely won her into freedom. In her last letter she writes of having prepared a thanksgiving list (the best medicine for attacks of grumbling!)—"I have prepared quite a big one and am putting in more and more heads". Does that seem very pedestrian? St. Paul who was a very experienced missionary would not have thought so. Indeed, in his letter to the Christians of Colossae, Chapter 3, verses 12-17 (not forgetting verse 1) he seems to have put forward almost exactly the same prescription.

Yet another freedom is freedom from "the narrow legalistic and petty justifications of the 'Law' into a realization of the wideness, sincerity, and the self-knowledge of the grace of Christ. Many times converts have tried to express to me what they felt as the difference, and usually it could be included in the words 'inner sincerity' in all relationships with God and neighbour, rather than the outward observance of the law".

There are echoes there of the Epistle to the Galatians. The missionary who wrote those words was referring to converts from Islam. But legalism is not a monopoly of Jews and Muslims. Christians wander in that same wilderness almost as easily. There is after all no clear line which separates the Pharisee and the Publican. A justified publican can very easily become a Pharisee. Part of the missionary task, perhaps the hardest part of all, is telling that truth in the wilderness and remaining humble in the telling.

But we are not only saved *from* sin, and fear and death, from being negative or pharisaical, from being lost in the howling waste of the wilderness: we are saved *into* a new kind of life. We enter a new circle. That is a good analogy. For in a very real sense we become free of the world. It was a very shrewd and experienced missionary in India, one with no illusions whatever either about foreign missionaries or about the Church in India who said: "The Church represents 'the open society' in India, that India which is the country of closed societies all of them trying to maintain their own cultures and ways of thinking." He added as an afterthought "Christ has a hard task". Is there anything more essentially lonely or lost than a closed society, or a closed mind? Christ goes out into the wilderness to find those who are lost like that. And his Church, with many stumblings, is following him there on the same mission.

The en-circling of the closed mind takes many forms. But the first step is always to make sure one is in the circle oneself. Only as part of the circle can you take part in en-circlement. That is one reason why in relation to Muslims for instance a new conscience is at work among many missionaries seeking to ensure that their own minds are open, that their presence in the Muslim world is a loving presence, that when they stand at the doorway of the Household of Islam and utter the greeting 'Peace . . .' they know in whose Name they utter it and what manner of spirit they are of (*St. Luke* 9. 55). Conferences in which Christians and Muslims have shared in Ibadan, Jerusalem, Beirut, Isfahan and Lahore mark a new determination by Christians, and perhaps a new readiness by Muslims, to take fresh looks at each other.

There remains one great new area of freedom to which we must refer, the world of a new relationship between man and wife. Here are two short conversation pieces, one from Africa and one from Asia.

"'She will be quicker than me'—a Nuba Christian was speaking of his wife. We were talking about fitting words to local tunes and learning to play a recorder. The remark surprised me. It was unusual for a man to speak in such a way of his wife; a man too with ability in singing and one who has composed some Nuba hymns.

"'We husbands and wives are trying out a new thing,' he said. 'It is a way of partnership and we cannot go back to the old way.' In the old way the wife is treated like a slave and, if she fails to do what is expected of her, her husband beats her. 'We cannot do this,' he said. 'If we see something wrong we must speak about it openly, and she must be ready to listen and look at the truth. We too are ready for her to speak to us.'"

The continual drag back of the old ways and deep-rooted traditions remains, but the en-circling has begun.

From India comes the next one.

"There is Phoebe calling. She has come with her husband to visit us. She tells us excitedly of her new home, the first she has ever known because she was an orphan and brought up here. Her husband joins in the conversation and tells us proudly of how Phoebe is looking after the headmaster's children—a task she is well fitted for because she used to help in the nursery here. They sound so happy together. Who are they? Only a servant and his bride? No. A Christian partnership!"

> *Yonder a maid and her wight*
> *come whispering by :*
> *War's annals will cloud into night*
> *ere their story die*[1]

Thomas Hardy was right. This is where romance spells reality. And at the heart of this reality stands the Christ who is setting men and women free all over the world —free for fellowship, free together to turn the wilderness into a garden.

And another little unnoticed revolution is taking place in the world of womanhood, where freedom has other challenges—"Dorcas was the only member of her family to be 'saved', and all the rest took the oath in

[1] From the poem "While Nations Pass", by Thomas Hardy.

the early days of Mau Mau. When her brothers tackled her, she gave them her testimony—her only weapon. In exasperation, they hired a car and one night took her down to the plains towards the Kamba country to a 'doctor' (i.e. tribal medicine man) to exorcise the Christian spirit from her. She had no idea where she was going or what it was about until in the firelight of his hut she saw the doctor, and was left with him. At once she gave her testimony, after which he was quiet for some time. Then he called her brothers. 'I can do nothing with the girl,' he said, 'take her away.' They were furious at the wasted effort and expense, and beat her, with no effect; she would not take the oath. Finally they said 'There's only one thing to do with you; we'll arrange things to keep you quiet'. And they took her away to the home of a Mau Mau supporter up near the forest line, and married her to him as a sub-sidiary wife. When he took her into the room later, she gave him her testimony, and said 'The thing is evil, for you and your own wife. I will not willingly be your wife'. At which he was very angry and thrashed her, stripped her of all her clothes, and tethered her to a stake outside by a rope round her neck, and left her there all night tied up like a goat. It was very cold, and in the morning some brethren found her there, and took her home, and cared for her. Emancipated womanhood? I wish you could see her."

Can we or can we not see the desert beginning to blossom like the rose?

F O U R

The Lord will comfort Zion; he will comfort all her waste places, and will make her wilderness like Eden, her desert like the garden of the Lord.   ISAIAH 51. 3

A WILDERNESS, at first sight, is a very unpromising place. It is not that nothing grows there, but that what does grow seems so stunted. It is not that nothing lives there but that what does live lives so precariously. One knows just why the prophet described the just ruler who gives his people security as being "like streams of water in a dry place, like the shade of a great rock in a weary land" (*Isaiah* 32. 2). A desert makes one tired and thirsty. Life in a desert offers no margins, and it is the margins of life that make for well-being, for joy, for the abundant life, for the overflow of energy which makes creative action possible.

For the vast majority of mankind life is dragged out in 'waste places', materially waste very often and no less often spiritually waste. That surely was one reason why the people of God in the Old Testament, not only in their beginnings, wandered in a wilderness—but even when they reached the promised land they lived always on the edge of the wilderness, within the threat of the wilderness. If their experience of God was to be relevant to all mankind it had to be a wilderness experience.

But what was the experience? The song of Moses in *Deuteronomy* 32 is worth a lot of meditation, one clue to its meaning being the frequent reference to God as the Rock of his people—not just a protection but the source of water. The song begins with words which are echoed in the text at the head of this chapter.

"Give ear, O heavens, and I will speak; and let the earth hear the words of my mouth. May my teaching drop as the rain, my speech distil as the dew, as the gentle rain upon the tender grass, and as the showers upon the herb. For I will proclaim the name of the Lord. Ascribe greatness to our God."

That is the proclamation—a telling in the wilderness. It is the promise that the waste places will be 'comforted', that the wilderness will become like Eden, the desert like the garden of the Lord.

We therefore accept the way through the wilderness, refuse to be daunted by the desert, treat the waste as a challenge. God is in the wilderness: he leads through the wilderness: he can transform the wilderness: he is the God of 'happening', things happen because the Spirit of God is at work. He is the coming One, the One who becomes more and more visible to those who have eyes to see. In that glorious certainty a Christian can say of the new life bursting out of the desert—"Not that I have already obtained this or am already perfect; but I press on to make it my own". That is the humble, realistic, hopeful way to look at the missionary movement of our time, at the Church overseas, and the Church at home, and the parish in which we live.

Let us begin with a disaster, the kind of disaster, incidentally, which can happen in a desert when a sudden storm of rain turns a dry watercourse into a raging torrent sweeping all before it. Something like that happened to the Indian village of Jeyi in the Uttar Pradesh not so long ago. The mud houses of the little Christian school collapsed one after another after a tremendous flood. For a short time 150 people were packed like sardines into a six-roomed bungalow. And even after most had been evacuated eleven of the second-year students contrived to share the house with two missionaries.

The flood was a real disaster. "What was the result of this life of unconscious identification, which was none of our doing?" asks one of those who experienced it. "We did not realize that anything was happening at the time, but afterwards we began to realize that a relationship of mutual trust, understanding and courtesy had grown up, which goes much deeper than the normal student-teacher relationship." St. Paul once wrote to some friends of his in the first of all 'younger churches' —"My little children, with whom I am again in travail until Christ be formed in you" (*Galatians* 4. 19). The 'formation of Christ', his becoming in us, takes time. Unexpected disasters often help.

A letter from Northern Nigeria tells of work by a doctor and his wife in a remote village community of pagan Hausas which can receive only occasional visits. The writer speaks of the immense difficulty of getting the men to change their attitude to their womenfolk. The last chapter in this book spoke of the revolution already taking place in this respect in many places. But elsewhere it moves slowly, and nowhere more slowly than in this part of Nigeria. "If one talks to the men about their wives many are not aware that anything needs changing. Those that see the need to lighten the women's lot do not see how they can do so, as they feel that once they have made their wives' lives easier the wives will become lazy and do no work at all (*a very masculine argument!*)." The writer adds this comment. "Any change in the present set-up in the near future will be just as much due to the coming of

46

Christ into the lives of the Christians and especially the Christian families as was their original conversion." The thoughtful reader will reflect that that conclusion has a relevance wider afield than that remote Nigerian village.

The coming of Christ, his 'becoming' in us and in the life of the Church, can be looked at upon a wider canvas, and here I would take the reader to South India. We under-estimate the importance of Church Union there, perhaps even fail to understand one of the reasons why it happened, if we do not take into account the actual condition of the Christians there before the union, and of their continuing condition still. What follows is a very frank appraisal by one who has identified himself with these Christians. He is viewing the situation from 'within'. We can read what follows only if we take note of a sentence by the writer with which his account ends. "In fact living in Tinnevelly is not unlike living in Victorian England." My only quarrel with that is that he might just as well have said 'Elizabethan' England, and by that I mean the England of the second Elizabeth!

Writing of a well-established community of one hundred years' standing in the Diocese of Tinnevelly he says: "It has many imperfections—some purely nominal Christians, a traditionalist and conservative outlook among the majority, factions, unchristianized areas of their life, such as caste prejudice, the dowry system, black marketing. Over against these a newly evangelized community of the same size is more hopeful and attractive. The situation is fluid in the latter and things are happening. All this goes to demonstrate the truth that every generation of Christians needs to be converted afresh, and that we do not get near fulfilment in the *Parousia* by the passage of time, except nearer to judgment" (*a very important observation*). "And yet it is also true that even the most unsatisfactory older Christian community has immensely greater resources both for self-renewal and for making an impact on society than a new-born one. One thinks particularly in Tinnevelly of our great enterprise of Christian education and all that it has meant both in giving a Christian education to non-Christians, the fruits of which are still to come, and in training Christian leaders in various walks of life. The general picture of development gives one hope that the leaven will go on working whatever crises and setbacks we may still have to meet."

After querying "whether as yet we have done more with the bulk of our Church membership than convert them from paganism to a Christianized brand of Judaism, or rather one of several denominational brands" (a remarkable echo, by the way, of the situation revealed in St. Paul's letter to the Galatians) he continues that nevertheless "Christ has come and Christ is preached and believed and that makes the difference".

The Rock is there with them in the wilderness. The Rock is following them through the wilderness. The Rock is Christ. The same "supernatural drink" (1 *Corinthians* 10. 4) which was available in the wilderness of long ago is available in the wilderness still—water to drink and also water to make a garden out of the waste.

Here is a glimpse at another part of the sub-continent, from Pakistan. The groups of our fellow-Anglicans whom it describes are members of a 'sweeper' community, desert dwellers with a vengeance. A letter from this community has the following description of how hard it is to see the coming of the Christ. "We are for the most part an illiterate community to which the Bible, the prayer book, and the hymn book are still largely closed books. In a similar situation to ours

48

the Roman Catholics teach the use of the rosary; the holy picture and the crucifix serve both as a means and a centre for some sort of daily family worship. But when we turn to see what the Protestant Church is doing in this matter of helping her people make real the presence of Christ in personal devotion we find that almost everything she has to offer is directed towards the literate. Our Christ is the Christ met once a week in Urdu Matins. Is it therefore to be wondered at that such a Christ is not meeting the deep spiritual needs of our folk? Nor will he, until we find some way of making him the Christ who can be met day by day within the milieu of our illiterates' one-room world."

The unfinished task of the unformed Christ. The morning I wrote these words I had earlier used this prayer. Perhaps we can make it our own as an act of faith for ourselves and for these Christians in Peshawar.

Because thou art my Father, I am not afraid. Because it is thine own Spirit that stirs within my spirit's inmost room, I know that all is well. What I desire for myself I cannot attain, but what thou desirest in me thou canst attain for me. The good that I would I do not, but the good that thou willest in me, that thou canst give me power to do.
Amen. Come Lord Jesus.

Our thoughts must stretch themselves further still if we are to be truly expectant of the Christ who is still to come. One missionary writes: "Shortly before I left Westcott House in November 1947 to come out to South India to be ordained in the C.S.I., Dr. Raven said that all his life he had waited in vain for a great formative theologian to arise in India to interpret St. John's Gospel to the world." He then goes on to describe efforts being made to set Indians free to think and write, and adds: "This illustrates the 'Christ who is yet to come', for the Indian Church is so far stunted by its failure to interpret the Gospel in the light of its special genius."

The same is true of every country in Asia without exception. In Africa there is a slowly dawning awareness that the Christ has still to become fully incarnate there. And in part, as we saw in Chapter One, the very western-ness of the dress in which the Gospel has been proclaimed and the Church built up is an obstacle. There was a sense of this behind the remark of a young African: "We must get back, for our people, behind the form of western Christianity which you have brought us, to the real thing."

Perhaps the most searching and daunting question facing Church leaders in Africa, and especially foreigners, is "Are we prepared to take the risk of the REAL as he is revealed to the African?" The risks to our westernized Church fabric will be tremendous, let there be no doubt about that. But the risks of refusing the Africans' own interpretation may be even more devastating.

Meanwhile something is 'happening' beyond our human expectations and we in England may be more closely involved than we realize. This extract from a recent letter is intriguing.

"I was in London for a meeting with a young Acholi pastor who is doing a post-ordination course at St. Augustine's. We met another Acholi—the first of his tribe to be reading law—and he took us to his room in Mutesa House. There we sat on his bed and drank lemonade, while he played a tape-recording of his translation and setting of Christmas carols, and we discussed the theology of calling not 'all the faithful' to worship him, but, as he had put it, 'all you Acholi, Alur, Madi, Jaluo, and other related Nilotic tribes' to adore him! Meanwhile another Acholi had arrived—a teacher taking his diploma at Edinburgh, also another, the first of his tribe to study for his Fellowship at the Royal College of Surgeons. Sharing a room with the law student was another who had just graduated in agriculture and was on his way back to Uganda, while later another came in, arrived that day by air from Chicago where he had just taken his degree in dentistry. Each of them was the first of this tribe in their professions—except the pastor and the teacher."

The Acholi would certainly appear to be going places! Have any of them come to your church? Has your parish ever invited a party of foreign students for a visit? Have you had an African or an Indian, a Chinese or a Japanese, in your home?

A missionary from Nigeria writes of a new bit of initiative being undertaken in the school where she is working: "It was started by one of our African staff just back from England." Attributing this fresh initiative to new visions caught in England, she goes on: "The work that is being done for the Nigerian Church by the Church in England cannot be over-estimated. Over and over again we see the spiritual temperature of the church the student has attended reflected on his return. Sometimes it gives us cause for great joy; sometimes we are disappointed."

What a shattering challenge! Apart from the question of the church boiler, is the *temperature* of your church at freezing point or blood heat? Africans and Asians feel the 'cold' very much indeed. Look to it.

There are other ways in which we still have to wait for his coming. Love of power rather than the power of love corrodes the life of the Church in every land. The following happens to have an African address but that is of no significance.

"I think of many hours spent in discussion with two leading African clergy in respect of a teacher in their area who they felt to be flouting their authority. As their fellow one stood alongside them in the problems of their ministry, but one had also to stand against them in insisting that spiritual authority could not be wielded like temporal, and that their only power ultimately to win the obedience and respect of the teacher concerned was the power of love. It must be accepted," he goes on sadly, "that on this particular occasion one appeared to fail completely, and the clergy remained quite unconvinced that only by the losing of their lives in the voluntary giving up of their authority would they gain them in the free allegiance of the teacher responding to their love and care." Concealed in that extract is another of the gravest problems confronting the Church in Africa, and one of the most serious threats to its growth.

Out of the depths of his experience St. Paul could disclaim having come anywhere near perfection. He acknowledged that he knew as yet only "in part". A missionary recently wrote in mordant vein: "In education we struggle with the half-educated, the half-knowledgeable, the half-trained, and especially some who cannot see that they are only half-something." That is a mirror we all have to hold up to ourselves till the Christ who is not yet formed in us has fully come into his own.

At this point we may perhaps ask ourselves if the foreigner has any real place in the Christian mission of our time. Already on earlier pages some answers to that question will have been discovered. What follows is I think an important part of the answer, and it applies of course to all foreigners whatever the colour of their skin, or the background from which they come.

"One of the greatest contributions of the missionary," says a writer, "is just to be the sand in the oyster shell. Being the sand involves one in experiencing the sharp edges, the angles, and the tensions of the incarnational life, and then of facing the cost and involvement of bringing that experience into the experience of one's African brethren. The grain of sand has to produce a reaction, and to be itself wrapped up in the perfection which God will create, being in the process unwanted and its contribution unknown."

St. Paul did not only say that he was not perfect. That was a glimpse of the obvious. But he went on to say: "I press on to make it my own, because Jesus Christ has made me his own" (*Philippians* 3. 12). That is our joyful assurance. Christ Jesus has made us his own, and he will most certainly complete the good work he has begun. This chapter can perhaps best end by us all sitting at a parochial church council meeting in Southern Sudan.

"Sitting in the local church council meeting on a hard bench for hours on end one sees and hears all kinds of things. If one thought only of the weaknesses, and there are many and grave ones—failures in steward-ship of money here, someone taking a second wife there, a teacher losing interest, etc. etc.—one would think that it was all hopeless; but when one remembers the other half of *Philippians* 3. 12 'Jesus Christ has made *us* his own' there are many signs to show that he is working in spite of the weaknesses. People are turning to the Lord in great numbers; albeit for many it is not a very intelligent turning, but thank God it is his evaluation and not ours that counts."

"In the Fellowship meeting one Friday afternoon Pastor looked around and said 'We are here today as the result of other people's prayers. Missionaries and others in the past have longed and prayed for there to be such a group and now their prayers are being answered—let us not forget that our prayers may take years before the answer comes but it will come."

Let us pray "*Amen. Come Lord Jesus*".

F I V E

A voice cries: "In the wilderness prepare the way of the Lord, make straight in the desert a highway for our God".

ISAIAH 40. 3

THE wilderness has a variety of its own. Here it may be open steppe, hard-baked earth with scattered clumps of dried-up scrub: elsewhere rolling hills of hard sand, with slabs of rock breaking the surface: again it may be dried-up bush, yellow and dead from the sun glare yet in its very deadness a memory and a promise of life: sometimes it will be a wild-looking land of boulders and outcrops of granite: but always a harsh and cruel land, a barrier to be forced, an obstacle to communication, something savage and untamed. It is here in this wilderness that we are to prepare a way through, a means of travelling, and the first steps towards settlement and the transformation of the waste.

A first step before any road can be built is the making of an accurate survey. What is the land really like? What is the prospect of water, are there minerals, is there oil? These and a hundred other questions will determine the kind of road that will be built. It is not so very different when we come to explore the wilderness of human life. Our first task is to make a survey and with that survey this chapter will be concerned.

In the 'enquiry' which has produced letters from so many parts of the world I listed four possible spiritual landscapes about which I wanted information, four kinds of wilderness, four 'worlds' if you like. I wanted to know what evidence there was of a 'world' which has not so much as heard whether there is a Christ.

Again I wanted evidence of a 'world' in which even if known he has been completely misunderstood. Then, third, I asked about the 'world' into which the Christ has come and provoked a response, maybe of acceptance, maybe of rejection, maybe a mixture of both. Finally I asked for evidence of any 'world' which had known him, accepted him, and then rejected him. It seemed to me that the highway for our God would have to be built through landscapes made up from all of these and who knows what other strange configuration of the human heart.

The replies were most illuminating. I like this bit of survey from Sudan and not least the 'vision' implicit in it, a refusal to treat any of it as belonging to the 'never never'. "We cannot forget," writes this surveyor, "that he is already there himself, in person, in the four 'worlds' which you list. They are his worlds, created and sustained by him. Because of that, these four worlds are not what they appear to be on the surface, but in reality are worlds where Christ is *now* redeeming and remaking men.

"You asked of the 'world' which has not heard of Christ: I thought here of the yet unevangelized area of the North and the pagan areas of the South. Darfur, our north-westerly province, has as far as I know no Christian witness within it. Again within one hundred miles of Mundri, in three different directions are pagan tribes with no literature at all, and a very small number of Christian members, mostly if not all, schoolboys or ex-schoolboys. Or I thought also of the cattle camps of such tribes as the Dinka where Christ is but rarely preached, and where even yet there is no indigenous form of worship adapted to the peculiar circumstances of their nomadic way of life.

"Then there is the 'world' in which Christ has

provoked a response both for and against him: here I thought at once of a journey north from Juba on the post-boat. I tried to talk to some of the Muslim sailors, and to give them some tracts, but one felt all the time that for them, at any rate, the question was settled and Christ rejected. There seemed to be no way of breaking in, and I shall never forget the look of almost scorn with which one man, his beads in his hand, brushed aside the Gospel which one of his friends, to whom I had given it, was showing him."

The same surveyor suggests another 'world'—"the 'world' where Christ seems irrelevant". "I thought," he writes, "of the 'Native Lodging Area', or *mulukia*, in Juba. A bustling, noisy, crowded area of African huts, with beershops all too evident—small 'buses coming and going and the market always busy. I stood in the market once selling tracts and, with our students, have passed through the lanes and paths trying to talk to the people. Some we brought to church, but somehow one felt all too painfully how irrelevant our little coloured booklets, and our 'message of an afternoon' must seem to the people of that city."

This sense of apathy weighs heavily on another in whose survey, also from Sudan, occurs the following passage. "To the community Christ has been both represented and misrepresented. I know of no one who is a non-Muslim in this particular area who is genuinely antagonistic towards him although many are apparently apathetic. I say apparently because I think that their apathy is partly our fault. People flock in to be baptized, they flock to a convention or to any open-air preaching. They gather round when our evangelist goes visiting, yet for most of them, baptized or not, the beer huts are a more usual gathering place than the church on Sunday. He is not unknown, he has not been rejected, he has not been accepted and rejected (with individual exceptions). I believe that he is deeply desired at this time but that (a) he has been and is misrepresented and his yoke made to appear ill-fitting and his burden heavy and (b) that the desires of the flesh particularly attractive here at this time make men inclined to be like the young Augustine—desperately desiring the fuller life in Christ but not prepared to make the break."

Later in the same letter there is a passage about the need to show "that Christ's life really is a fuller one and not the dull, grey thing that every village church Sunday morning service portrays".

Getting the right road levels in Sudan is obviously difficult.

Iran provides a supplement. Having spoken of "the villagers and tribal people among whom almost nothing is known of Christ" the surveyor's report goes on: "In this 'world' Christ has been misrepresented by Islamic misunderstandings of Christian doctrine," and he adds: "The historical sense of these people has been tele-scoped, as it were, and to them the Crusades were only yesterday. The Crusades have left a bitter scar on all Islamic people, who still regard the Christian as an enemy, and Christianity as western."

That is indisputable. But the cambering of the road through the Islamic world is going to be extremely difficult because the Christianity seen in the Muslim world is so often Christianity *plus* or Christianity *minus*. From Jordan comes this comment. "The 'world' we move in is that of a more or less educated and largely secularized Christian and Christian-influenced Muslim section of Arab society. It is a world that knows about Christ, that admires Christian ethics (without neces-sarily acknowledging them as Christian) and that is underneath often religious, but does not altogether know Christ as a person."

That word 'secular' is a reminder that there is one factor common to all these worlds and that is the sudden and devastating impact of our modern world of technology, mass media of communication, and materialistic values upon old systems of thought and ancient patterns of procedure. Everywhere in Asia and Africa two world-views are in collision.

There is an almost unbearable pathos in this poem of a young West African woman, already familiar to those who have seen the C.M.S. film, *Hanging in the Middle Way*.

> *Here we stand,*
> *infants overblown*
> *poised between two civilizations*
> *finding the balance irksome*
> *itching for something to happen,*
> *to tip us one way or the other,*
> *groping in the dark for a helping hand*
> *and finding none.*
> *I am tired, O my God, I am tired,*
> *I am tired of hanging in the middle way,*
> *But where can I go?*[1]

That cry goes for many. The whole purpose of a Christian education in Africa and Asia is to provide for such a highway in the desert. But unfortunately the road builders are in very short supply. At the end of that great vision of the Highway in *Isaiah*, chapter 35, come the words of fulfilment "they shall obtain joy and gladness, and sorrow and sighing shall flee away" (v. 10). How wonderful it will be to hear "the shout of them that triumph, the song of them that feast", but that

[1] From *Conflict* by Mabel Imoukhuede.

is not yet. We are not entitled to that enjoyment as long as young Africa can say "I am tired, O my God, I am tired", as long as there is no road with a signpost telling them where to go.

No road! At once we find our minds leaping to the 'dead end' of those millions of refugees for whom there are no signposts just because there are no roads. In this World Refugee Year we are being forcibly reminded that there is no harsher or more tragic wilderness than that of the refugee, the man, the woman, the child—without home and without hope. Tired? Oh, my God, how tired!

In prose and not in poetry this comes from East Africa: "There are no 'pure pagans' or 'primitive pagans' here for the simple reason that animism as a whole way of life has long since broken down. Now we have pagans whose 'world picture' is a confused mass of ancient and modern. Many have lived for years away from the Reserve—in the Big City or on European farms. Their religion is materialism, politics, and no one knows what kind of witchcraft, all mixed up together." The writer adds: "I have not met anyone who denies that God is, but the idea of God is pretty remote from life."

"Pretty remote from life." You do not have to go to Nairobi to glimpse that 'world' without God. You don't have to leave the 'four-mile radius', the Bull Ring in Birmingham, Princes Street in Edinburgh, or College Green in Dublin to know that for most people God is "pretty remote from life". Road building for God in the wilderness today is everywhere as tough an assignment as it must have seemed to Isaiah in his darker moments or to John the Baptist later on.

In the Niger Delta area, formed by the silt carried down by the river, there is no local stone. It all has to be imported if you want to make a road. That is a parable of the missionary job everywhere today, in Britain as much as elsewhere. Local materials and local man-power are *nowhere* adequate by themselves. That is perhaps the first most important fact that is yielded by our preliminary survey.

For good measure let me give this thoughtful assessment in a survey sent in from India. Analysing the various local factors our surveyor writes as follows: "The battle for India's soul is doubtless being fought not so much in the Church's specific pastoral and evangelistic work, though these have their place in the warfare, still less in the Church's often petty politics; but rather in the great nation-wide upheaval both positive and negative, at the impact of western society both in its Christian and sub-Christian aspects."

Our surveyor has got himself involved here in military metaphors. But perhaps it does no harm to remember that our road building is not just a shifting of material obstacles, but contending with "spiritual wickedness". We build under fire.

Perhaps this bit of investigation which began with a poem from a young West African woman can be closed with the remark of a schoolgirl from East Africa. It too has its pathos though of a rather different kind. To those who know 'the world's slow stain' and also the overwhelming pace of change in the midst of which we live this schoolgirl's question will not be lacking in urgency: "How can a person control herself to be humble before God, when the world is so full of wonderful things of man's invention?" Christian schools exist to give the answer but, as I indicated earlier, a voice is required for the telling of the answer. And the voices are all too few. To return to our metaphor, you cannot build roads without a labour force.

There is a 'wilderness' of human life created by deliberate rejection of Christ. The road here advances only inch by inch. From Kashmir comes a picture of outright rejection. A health centre was offered to a certain village, already notorious in the records of the little Christian hospital for the shocking condition of so many maternity cases for whom nothing had been done or the wrong things done before resort to the hospital became necessary to save life. The health centre would have made all the difference. The government officials concerned were helpful. Kashmiri Christians were ready to start work. European help was available. But the fanatical hostility of the villagers to any help from Christians was maintained unbroken. How much tragic misunderstanding lies behind that rejection!

A builder on that bit of the road writes of this rejection: "'Ye will not come unto me that ye might have life'—those were the words which came often to my mind, and somehow I was able to glimpse a fraction of what the world's rejection of himself must mean to Christ. To have, through God's grace and love, the power to heal, the knowledge to pass on whereby tragedy could be averted and sickness prevented, and to see and hear the people deliberately reject it all, was heartbreaking and yet, as one had gone at the call of Christ, he gave enrichment as one was led in a new way into the fellowship of his sufferings."

We have here been much concerned with the wilderness. It is good to be reminded from Kashmir as we were earlier from Sudan that the Lord for whom we prepare the way is not waiting for us to finish it but is our fellow-Workman.

There is just room for a glimpse at two other bits of landscape. The first comes from Japan. A schoolgirl is speaking. For years she has been desperately engaged in passing examinations—there is an education fever in Japan every whit as pressing as anywhere in Africa. After she had passed into senior high school it seemed to the Japanese rector of her parish church that now was the time to prepare her for confirmation. When her father told her this she replied: "Why should I be confirmed? Why should I waste time going to church? Life is too short for anything but the most important things, and church is not one of those. Study is the only really important thing and I shall continue to study. You had no business to have me baptized if this means that I have to waste valuable time in useless worship."

You can almost see that schoolgirl in her tantrum. I give the illustration only because busyness and especially busyness over study is a major obsession in Japan today, posing tremendous problems for the Christian Church. Perhaps this busyness is in part an expression of that tremendous anxiety which is spreading over the world, a half-conscious fear that unless we hurry up we shan't have time to live. For this same pressure is invading other parts of the world and is certainly not peculiar to Japan. But no less certainly does it help to create a wilderness for the human spirit everywhere. Such busyness does not help with the building of what the Americans call a 'thruway'.

Spending as I do a large part of my time in an office, and trying not to create too much of a wilderness for my office staff, I cannot forbear to close this chapter with an illustration from office life! It can be a wilderness life as thousands know in our western world. And this peculiar form of existence is being introduced by us everywhere else.

This letter comes from a missionary society's office in Nairobi and speaks of the numbers of boys, and some girls, who become junior clerks, typists and office boys. "These," says the writer, "have had some schooling, probably only about six years, and most likely have failed to get a place in a senior secondary school. They will never become 'intelligentsia' in the true sense of the word, though some may become political or other leaders of the half-educated type. Some are good stuff, but have not had the opportunity of further schooling. They will become an essential part of the civil service and business world, doing the humdrum work of typing and filling in forms. There must be millions of their counterparts in all parts of the world. As modern business methods become more and more mechanized, their job becomes more impersonal and deadening. With the increasing use of dictaphones the typist may not even see her boss, only hear a mechanical voice coming through the earphones. Many of these young-sters have been taught in Christian schools. They have heard of Christ. They may not have any desire to reject him: but what connection has he with this mechanized office work? We fail to proclaim Christ in the office as Lord of machines and of men, and to offer him the fruit of our labour there."

She adds: "What have we as a Christian office to proclaim by word and way of life to the commercial firms around us? We hope that we do treat all as persons, not things; but we have a lot to learn about Christ as the Head of the office."

A consecrated typist, as I have good reason to know, is as important for the building of the road as any of the other workmen. On, then

to the bound of the waste,
On, to the city of God

64

S I X

IF we are to prepare the way of the Lord in the wilderness we must, as we have seen, survey the land in which the highway has to be built. We have to be very clear about the obstacles we shall meet, the difficulties we shall encounter. We have the highest authority for sitting down to count the cost before beginning to build anything. That done, however, we need to be clear about the underlying principles of our craft. Later we shall be looking at actual methods of operation. But behind any method, if it is to be successful, there must be the right principles. If you are a carpenter you do your best work *with* the grain not *against* it. If you are building a road you have to take into consideration subsoil, water levels, and contours. Your road is related to these. So it is in the task of 'telling in the wilderness' the good news about God.

Nothing is more remarkable in the long wilderness wanderings of the people of Israel than the grace which they found in the wilderness. This, of course, is part of the meaning which must be recognized in that picture of the 'moving Rock' which so caught the imagination of their poets.

With that grand assurance, itself the very heart of the good news which we have to tell, it is possible to recognize what is the *first* great principle of telling, of proclamation—expectancy. That is the great positive

65

quality of faith. Faith in the Bible is not the quality of submission but of co-operation, not of acquiescence in the unpredictable but of commitment to the known. You put your trust 'into' Someone, and you expect the answer, not necessarily the answer you want but the answer which will be just right in those circumstances. You know the answer will be right because you know the Person who gives the answer. This, then, is the first great principle of our telling, that we shall expect great things from God.

That notable missionary William Carey knew that that was the point of beginning for the 'Mission'. It is because we expect great things from God that we can attempt great things for him.

The greatest thing we can expect is 'grace in the wilderness', grace for the moment, grace to do the next thing. That is the grace-faith relationship which working out in small things and in big means salvation.

Here we see it in action at a very humble level in Kenya. "In Mombasa," writes a doctor, "there is a railway draughtsman, a leader of the 'brethren'. Always cheery, with his whole life a witness to the grace of God, he is constantly on the move in his spare time, linking up with other Christian groups, and being a continual inspiration to fellow-Christians, black and white." Back of that man's devotion is expectancy.

Here is another illustration from the same area, a man 'in the wilderness' finding grace and responding with expectancy: "Japhet used to be a Church evangelist. Since pastors' salaries were raised last year he has been 'axed', so now he has to farm to make ends meet, but he hasn't a word of complaint. He still teaches Scripture in the local school, takes church services, and preaches to pagan family groups every Sunday afternoon."

One more, still from the same area: "The local headmaster's wife here, who is an outstanding witness to her faith, has five small children, all with whooping cough at the moment. When Jean visited her yesterday she herself was not well, but remained serene. 'If I think only of the children I am troubled, but if I think of Jesus first and then of the children it is all right', which is typical of her."

You could hardly find three simpler illustrations of grace in the wilderness issuing in the life of faith, of expectancy. They are so simple that we don't have to live in the coastal province of Kenya to understand them. Having 'spare time', being 'axed', having children with whooping cough, are not uncommon experiences. And, praise the Lord, grace is not uncommon either, though there's nothing like enough expectancy about.

Expectancy, of course, often takes the form of prayer. It is one of the purest forms of expectancy to be in the wilderness of doubt and uncertainty and self-distrust, and at that point to pray. A young missionary was on her first assignment, a difficult one, and one in which many of those with whom she was to work didn't believe because they didn't understand—a daunting experience, don't you think? She prayed: "Let not the devil of confusion rob my soul of inward peace. Let my 'outgoing' in these weeks and months be simply that of walking with Jesus in quietness and contentment." Is there any better way of walking through the wilderness? Those who walk like that will have something to tell.

The *second* great principle that lies behind good telling is a natural sequel to expectancy—it is knowing how to listen. How very true to life everywhere is the experience of this missionary in Jordan: "Listening I am sure is one of the chief functions of the foreign missionary in the new set-up here. We have all found that our Arab colleagues in church or school come and talk about their problems. Mostly we don't (very often can't) give them answers, but they don't really want answers (they want to find their own). They just want someone to talk to who understands the situation, is not too deeply involved in it, and won't repeat what they have heard to the whole neighbourhood."

That brief comment incidentally is just one more subtle indication of the important continuing role of the *foreign* missionary, provided he or she knows how to listen. I remember once listening to a man for a whole hour without saying a word. At the end he said "I see". He had brought all his difficulties out into the open. All he needed was a listener. Because I kept my mouth shut that man was able to hear Christ answer his questions.

But for effective listening you must know the language of the speaker. And language means more than a command of vocabulary. A missionary in North India writes: "Somehow the missionary has to put himself in a position where he can, in sympathy and imagination, enter as fully as possible into the thinking and feeling of the people around him—and this of course means much patient listening, together with a good knowledge of the language, and also of the culture, customs and religion of those he hopes to serve; but more than this —he must not only listen, but also seek to relate what he hears and learns to the Gospel which he comes to proclaim. How can Christ's forgiveness come to *mean* something—to *convey* anything at all, in terms he or she will understand—to the peasant in the village, the sick old lady in the hospital, the student who is dissatisfied with his own faith? These are only questions, but much listening, and much imagination, is needed if they are to be fruitfully and effectively answered."

Listening involves more than vocabulary—it means, among other things, being able to listen-in to an idiom of living. Very forcefully one missionary writes from Kenya: "No missionary will really get to know what is happening in modern Kikuyu village life, until he goes and becomes a citizen of one." The same insistence comes from Malaya: "Living in the villages in small houses, not much better than the village houses, and sharing many of the same disabilities, such as lack of water and light, and curfew restrictions, has brought us near to the village people in a way that nothing else could. . . . Of course, such physical identification alone is not enough; some who live like that are still miles from true identification; but it is one essential element in it."

But village life is not the only kind of life. There is the surging life of the towns, and today one factor in that life is the passionate assertion of self-hood, of the right to self-respect, which is the drive behind so many manifestations of nationalism and racialism today. Listening-in to the voices of nationalism and racialism isn't easy. From Kenya comes this very thoughtful comment by an experienced missionary: "The biggest problem in identification comes in the political sphere. African nationalism grows apace. The desire is for majority power in the Legislative Council as soon as possible. How far can we go along with this aspiration, when objective criticism suggests that it is utterly premature? How far can we get a hearing for the Gospel unless we align ourselves much more closely with this political objective? This is one of the big questions to which the Church has no clear answer. If there is no real meeting here the recognized Churches may be by-passed by the Africa of the future."

We must not burke that question. It is very closely tied up with our ability to listen to what is being said by many Africans today. To refuse to listen is to be without any true knowledge of Africa. There is devastating truth in what Fr. Huddleston says in his preface to that disturbing book by an African, *Land of Sunshine*[1]: "For the European, the colonizer, the missionary, the trader, the greatest danger and delusion is the certainty that he *knows* Africa. It is this which makes him, often, so bitterly resentful of the 'outsider' who dares to criticize his handling of the problem. It is this, for instance, which makes the Government of the Union of South Africa walk out of the United Nations. 'We know the Native: you don't.' In fact, of course, the European in Africa, on the whole, is totally ignorant of the African, because the only context in which he 'knows' him is the context of master-servant. It is precisely this ignorance, this blind, determined ignorance of the African *as a person* which, in the end, builds up into the appalling racial tensions which create the tragedy of Southern Africa today."

And not only *Southern* Africa. The biggest need of the white man everywhere in Africa is a hearing-aid. From every point of view it is indispensable for a missionary whatever the nature of the wilderness in which he has his message to tell.

There are still other kinds of listening we must recognize, for the Holy Spirit does not 'work to rule'. "I recall," writes a missionary from South India, "a Hindu student who had had a very deep experience of Christ as Saviour, coming often to tell me of his experiences. I frequently tried to urge him to face the question of baptism, but I was frequently rebuked by the evident way in which the Holy Spirit was leading him

[1] Muga Gicaru (Lawrence and Wishart Ltd., 1958).

forward; and leading him to face difficulties I was not really aware of. Particularly he wanted to show his parents, whom he dearly loved and who were obstructing him, that he was an obedient and not a deliberately disobedient son. He wanted if possible to win them. There is no doubt that his gentleness and goodness did a great deal to reconcile his parents to his decision, and he was finally baptized and confirmed. Where there is real experience the Holy Spirit is so often wiser than we." That discovery of grace came by listening!

And listening, genuine listening, must be our approach to other religious systems which claim the devotion of so many millions of our fellows. "I was visiting one of the largest shrines in Kyoto," writes a missionary from Japan, "and, after a conversation with the Chief Priest, I was taken by an assistant to see the inner part of the shrine. As we were sitting . . . I was questioned about our Christian understanding of God. . . . This would never have come about, if I had not gone first to ask and to learn." The same writer tells of a visit to the headquarters of one of the most vigorous Japanese religious sects and adds: "By going as a student, I have established intimate contact with a large number, and some of the younger professors at their university have dealt confidentially with their aspirations."

Listening is one form of the courtesy we offer to our fellow-men—and "the grace of God is in courtesy".

Listening, quite obviously, as several of the above illustrations have indicated, calls for imagination. And imagination is the *third* principle we need to grasp if we would tell our message so that those who hear will understand. And how very hard it is to be imaginative, especially with the unattractive! "I think," writes one missionary, "that at this point we are most often defeated by sophisticated young men. As one lives in a completely rural setting it is more and more easy to enter imaginatively into the prejudices, attitudes and fears of the people with whom one deals day by day. It is the young man in the white shirt, tie, suede shoes and sun glasses who swaggers up the road and condescends to greet his uncle and other senior relatives with an air of superiority that we find it most difficult to love imaginatively. My revulsion is, I am sure, based upon some fault in myself which I see reflected in him, and that is what blinds us most in our relationship with others. To put oneself in the position of the young schoolboy with all his superficial airs is our real challenge, and we cannot proclaim to him until we have so done. We sit where people sit day by day, we share our meals, our laughter and our sorrow—but the young man with the sun glasses stands and looks on. We are being called to stand where he stands, which is something he does not want and we are not inclined to do."

Imagination can be very costly. It can also be very rewarding. A missionary, much concerned with educational matters in a country recently become independent, tells of his experience. "I think of a headmaster, nervous and on the defensive at his first confrontation with a missionary on the specific subject of religion, the one a sincere Muslim, the other a sincere Christian. It was interesting to watch prejudice struggle with a sense of duty, and to feel the sense of being on trial. There was opportunity to sympathize with the practical problems of a headmaster, to get alongside him and share his burdens, to be understanding and not demanding. Then came the test of teaching day by day as a visiting member of staff, under the eye and ear of the same headmaster, with his eye on punctuality, his judgment of discipline and efficiency, of the quality of a lesson, and the interest and reaction of the boys. And as man got to know man, the beginnings of friendship, a cup of coffee together, the discussion of Middle East problems, the Christian approach to Islam and the Arab world—frontiers of understanding."

I am not surprised that that missionary could summarize his experience as a Christian educationist in the words, "By courtesy, by sincerity, by humility, by efficiency, by truth, by tolerance, by understanding, by genuine friendship and genuine service to the community, Christ is proclaimed." Is there an echo there of 2 *Corinthians* 6. 6–7? I think so. In that passage St. Paul was writing about some of the principles of proclamation.

Imagination can take so many forms. I suppose it represents the most important qualifications for a teacher. Have you ever tried to make 'All Saints' Day' come alive for a class of schoolgirls? I know a teacher who did it by writing a choral speaking 'pageant' for a form of African schoolgirls. The Chorus told the story of the Saints from St. Andrew to Apolo (a saint of the twentieth-century Church in Uganda). Each girl had five or six lines of her own. Here is part of the letter describing the 'pageant'. "The girl who was Paul described her reaction to Stephen, the Damascus road, etc., and ended 'I came to learn that nothing, nothing in life or death or the world to come, can separate us from the love of God which is in Christ Jesus our Lord'. She had to 'get it across' and she's one who has herself been medically under sentence of death. I wish you could have heard that 'nothing'. . . . I'm sure that for a few moments that evening we saw the glory of God in a little bit more of its all-embracing splendour."

The writer adds: "Whether all this is an example of

how those to whom you proclaim the Gospel proclaim it back to you; or whether it is an example of how God does his own work if you offer a bit of time and willingness, or whether it is a method of proclamation, I don't know, but I'm sure it has something to say." I'm sure it has—about the way of imagination.

Expectancy, listening, imagination, these three principles need for their energizing, if proclamation is to be effective—love. Let us begin at a very prosaic level. Here is a question out of Africa by a learner: "How much there is to learn!—loving people when they are arguing about their wages on pay-day, when they come with requests at the most inconvenient times, when through sheer laziness they let the ulcers on their children's legs get six inches long, when they steal, when they drive the baboons into another person's garden so that they will leave their own garden alone. What form does love take under these circumstances? What part does 'righteous indignation' or a severe rebuke have in love's working? These are lessons we are being called upon to learn in this place."

Another prosaic illustration comes from what is often a very prosaic place—the classroom. A missionary from Hong Kong writes of the temptation to which a missionary teacher is sometimes prone of grudging time spent on the chores of teaching which might be spent in developing personal contacts, and so in evangelism. The writer says: "I have been much exercised in my thought about this. I have come to see clearly that a missionary on the staff of a school must be prepared to have as full a time-table as the other Christians or non-Christians on the staff of the school. He must not be open to the criticism that I have heard 'to be a missionary is an easy job with less periods and fewer corrections'. The missionary must be prepared to witness through identification with all the problems of the busy teacher with a full time-table that Christ can save that situation too from overwork, tenseness, irritability and deadness. The missionary should be able to show that even in that situation he can still help his students both in class and out to understand more of this Way of Salvation which we proclaim."

That is love being very practical.

There are no easy answers. Love is a dimension of depth. We plumb the depth at very different levels. Only God has ever reached rock bottom.

One level which many have explored is that of just being a friend. A Muslim labourer working on the compound of a theological college in Nigeria was won for Christ simply by one of the students going out of his way to be a friend, first by 'showing an interest in his affairs', then by meeting his need in sickness, then by inviting him into his own home. One day in conversation the labourer started talking about religion. "He repeatedly mentioned the word 'love' in connection with Christianity." "Now," reports that student, "the way was open for the Gospel. . . . After careful reasoning together, my friend understood that Jesus Christ is the Son of God."

There is nothing that is not quite commonplace in that story, any more than there is in the story of a young man in Iran who when asked what made him first want to become a Christian replied: "Because I saw love in the life of another Christian. I watched him and I saw that all he did was activated by one motive, love—I too wanted to find the source of true love."

Rather devastating that—"I watched him". That thought ought to bring us to our knees.

"The nickname given to a missionary, 'the one who

talks', is not as rude as it sounds," writes one such talker, "when it means, as it does, 'the man who is always ready to talk to us'. In this sense it speaks of a communication of love successful in making a crossing-over between 'us' and 'them'. This involves giving up time in order to talk, and with the time a degree of efficiency, which is perhaps very dear to one's soul. Love of this kind is exposing, because in the talking there will be meeting—not on the superficial level of work and business, but on the deep levels of self-revelation."

Yes, "telling" sooner or later involves talking. But the talking, if it is talking the Gospel, is not just chatter. I find very helpful the following definition of what makes talk into "telling", which comes in a missionary's letter. He says "This is a rough list of what Evangelism means—

(a) The evangelist cares for the other *for his own sake*.
(b) He sees Christ as already loving and caring for the other person.
(c) He tries to understand the other's hopes, fears and inner longings, and the meaning of his situation.
(d) He translates his message so that the other may understand it easily.
(e) He allows the other time and opportunity to make his own decision."

That seems to me to be a very important definition of the principle of love in our proclamation.

And love for the Christian speaks fundamentally of *forgiveness*. Forgiveness is a principle which few of us find easy to understand. Most of us find it very easy to think that 'to forgive' and 'to let off' are the same thing. A missionary from Pakistan writes of an attitude of mind which he finds widespread "which regards

76

God's grace as 'cheap'—an attitude of 'too easy for-giveness' and a consequent lack of hatred for sin, and of the fear of God, and of the Christian obligation to obedience and working out of our salvation with fear and trembling". No doubt that attitude is very wide-spread in Pakistan. But one seems to have come across it just as often nearer home!

The real presentation of forgiveness is never easy, for we ourselves are so greatly in need of it. I confess to finding much wisdom in a letter from a missionary in Iran: "It is no use proclaiming Christ unless we first go down on our knees and ask the people we have wronged to forgive *us*! Our governments, our oil com-panies, and just people like me, by a superior attitude, have alienated our friends from Christ."

A Hindu student, a member of one of the reforming movements in Hinduism, said to one of our missionaries after visiting one of their centres, "What have you Christians to offer which we do not have here?" The missionary writes: "I pondered this question for long afterwards. It challenged me again and again in the pellucid 'goodness' of one of my Brahmin colleagues and in the spiritual aliveness of one of my Hindu students. I became convinced that the answer did not lie in moral values alone, not even in dogma. My search has not yet ended, but I feel that I have come some-where near the essential answer in characterizing Chris-tians in Father Andrew's words as 'the forgiven com-munity'."

It was an African, very conscious of being one of "the forgiven community", who was able to give this testimony from his own experience. "One day, when I had just finished taking a service in church, I came out to find that my little son had been speared. He was dying in his mother's arms while she was vainly trying to push back the intestines which were protruding from a gash in his abdomen. Two things were uppermost in my mind: distress at the loss of my only son, and fury against the perpetrator of the deed.

"'I must get away from myself and think this thing through before I do anything,' I thought, so I went right away and kneeled down to pray. At once I saw the Cross afresh, and my Saviour dying there for me, and then suddenly I realized something else: the anguish of God the Father at the death of his only Son, of whom *I* was the guilty murderer. I saw the spear wound in *his* side, and then I heard his voice saying, 'Father, forgive them, for they know not what they do'. I was quite broken down at the thought of what God had done for me, and all feelings of hate and bitterness for the man who had killed my son melted away, and in their place came an overwhelming sense of love. There and then I asked for forgiveness as I repented of the sin of hatred which had first flooded my soul, and then went back to the house to share with my wife what the Lord had been showing me.

"Meanwhile, the man who had speared the child had been caught. He was being held by a host of men all shouting at once, and holding spears, axes, knives, and bill-hooks, waiting for me, as father of the child, to give the word to despatch him. I walked up to them and told them to put their weapons down, then I said to the man, 'As God has forgiven me, so I forgive you'."

Grace in the wilderness!

S E V E N

He shall see the fruit of the travail of his soul and be satisfied.
ISAIAH 53. 11

The wilderness and the dry land shall be glad, the desert shall rejoice and blossom . . . . They shall see the glory of the Lord, the majesty of our God.
ISAIAH 35. 1, 2

THE goal of our proclamation is nothing less than the full satisfaction of Jesus Christ our Lord. And that as we know from the Epistle to the Ephesians is nothing less than our arrival up to "mature manhood, to the measure of the stature of the fulness of Christ" (*Ephesians* 4. 13). That would seem an ambitious goal enough. But the Bible is clear that God's purpose is wider still. The wilderness itself is to be redeemed and all who dwell in it. That is explicitly suggested in the tenth verse of the first chapter of the same Epistle. It is implied in our second text which introduces the great vision of the Prophet Isaiah. How all this will happen, and when, we do not know. But the Bible is clear enough that God intends his people to prepare for that day and that their obedience bears some relation to it. There is an intriguing passage in the Second Epistle of St. Peter whose meaning is not absolutely clear but which hints at this relation. The writer suggests that Christians ought to be noted for "lives of holiness and godliness", and then he continues, "waiting for and hastening the coming of the day of God" (2 *Peter* 3. 12). The New Testament contains another hint with the same bearing. In *St. Matthew* 24. 14 we read: "This

Gospel of the Kingdom will be preached throughout the whole world, as a testimony to all nations; and then the end will come."

An unconscious commentary on all this comes from an unlikely source. In 1954, at an international conference in Amsterdam, the distinguished English writer Charles Morgan spoke as follows: "The early Christians believed that the material world would end in their life-time. Science has given us a new reason for that belief. To them the shortness of the time was a means of grace; so may it be to us. It deprives materialism of its profit and tyranny of its power. It is an amnesty to all imprisonments of the mind, it empties out all the philosophies of disintegration. It is a reason to love and to be at peace."

As I say, that is an unusual commentary. Whatever our judgment upon it and upon the thought of 'hastening' the day of God, there is no doubt that the momentum of the missionary movement is decisively influenced by awareness of the goal. "The Kingdom of God," we know, "is righteousness and peace and joy in the Holy Spirit" and that "he who thus serves Christ is acceptable to God and approved of men. Let us then pursue what makes for peace and for mutual upbuilding" (*Romans* 14. 17–19).

Let us then pursue our goal knowing how momentous is our journey, how great our responsibility!

A very searching word which all in any way involved in the Christian Mission, at home or abroad, do well to heed, comes from a missionary in Eastern Nigeria. He writes: "Our Church membership certainly increases each year but one wonders how many have really been brought to a place of commitment. I was very surprised when conducting a mission in one of our large towns some time ago, at which a number of

80

prospective ordinands were helping us, to find that none of them knew what 'personal evangelism' meant until they were given some instruction in it while preparing for the mission. All of them had been catechists for some years! They were absolutely thrilled when as a result of their testimony and the moving of the Spirit in the hearts of their hearers, some young people openly professed conversion. These young catechists told me they had never experienced anything like it before."

The missionary then comments: "Somewhere in our missionary task out here we have failed them and maybe many others like them. Are we frightened of 'personal work' or have we no time for it? Our pastors, catechists and teachers are waiting to be given a lead. We seem to have lost the enthusiasm for evangelism that the early missionaries had, and we seem to be so busy 'administering' that the real purpose for our being here as missionaries in Nigeria is lost. I realize only too well that I am guilty in that I have neglected many such opportunities of witnessing for Christ. We need to recapture our vision of Christ's purpose for us as evangelists and be quite certain in our own minds that this is God's primary purpose for each one of us."

With that challenge before us we can without any sense of superiority consider this verdict on some of our fellow-Christians in one part of Sudan. Writes a missionary who has just returned from many years of service among the Dinka people: "Our Church in Sudan must be very like that which the writer to the Hebrews had in mind. The chief fault was that they had not yet perceived or experienced 'the something better' that God had for them. The majority of the Dinka Christians I know are still in that elementary stage of the Christian pilgrimage and have little desire to 'press forward' to the stage of full and perfect access to God through Christ."

I think that most of us will admit that we find it rather easy to 'settle down' in the wilderness at the very first oasis that we reach.

Personal commitment, personal holiness—these are indispensable steps towards the goal. But they cannot be pursued in isolation. It is in 'the forgiven community' and only in that company that the goal can be reached. "More and more care and thought," says a writer from Iran, "is being given to the proper 'grafting in' of the new branch into the Vine. The process depends on the very careful preparation of the convert for baptism, allowing a longer rather than a shorter time before baptism, whereby he or she can be absorbed in friendship and true fellowship into the new community." In Iran the Christian community is a small one and men and women join it one by one.

Elsewhere the picture may be different yet the principle is the same—the individual grows into and so grows in the Christian community. Some important reflections in this connection came in a letter from Uganda. "We have our Church in Uganda, some forty per cent of the population. What we have now to do is slowly to deepen its life. It will only be done eventually as a corporate act. I think that the recent Diocesan Mission showed that our Church can act as a body if sufficiently moved. Its need now is a deliberate, prolonged effort to take more seriously the demands of God in personal habits, in stewardship, and in fellowship. If the Church acts together the individual will not fear to move. If the Church corporately remains static, there will remain for the individual too vast a jump in going forward alone."

The writer then comments on the Revival Movement, that what happens there is that when an individual joins the group he leaves one society, his own, and becomes instead part of another. There is a real 'group' experience. The individual is never left alone. The writer adds: "The Revival shows what is needed in that its strength expresses itself in fellowship and togetherness. But those expressions of the life of Christ need to be seen in a wider fellowship within the whole Church, if Uganda's Christians are to go forward in the faith."

The goal beckons.

As I write I have in front of me an intriguing note in a letter from the Nupé country in Northern Nigeria. The writer says: "In all the villages round Bida the 'group' and 'community' is the operative unit. When I visit a village it is the *group* of Christians who decide which house I shall lodge in, what food shall be given to me, who is to sweep out the house and prepare it, and so on. No individual acts without the knowledge and consent of the group."

No doubt, in that instance, we are looking at a very simple level of social organization. Yet no Church, however developed, however intricately organized, can afford to do without these small nuclei of cohesion. It is one of the perennial problems confronting every Church, once it has grown to a considerable size, what to do with the 'little platoon' in which, when all is said and done, most of us are first brigaded. Far too little attention is paid to this problem, from which results directly the tragic tendency of great Churches to breed sects. A highly centralized Church can be as impersonal as a highly centralized business or a highly centralized bureaucracy. Perhaps a major preoccupation of every large Christian community ought to be to encourage the 'middle term' between the individual and the Church as a whole. The pursuit of holiness needs a concentration of energy. Concentrated energy is, of course, potentially explosive, but its dynamic can be harnessed to creative purposes. It is the wisdom of the great Church to see that this happens, for it has commonly been through the dynamism of a small group that holiness has made its impact on society outside the Church.

A shrewd awareness of this has brought together a group of Christian doctors and professors in a government medical college in South India to see how they can make their witness more effective in their professional work. A similar purpose characterizes the efforts of a growing number of such groups in many parts of the world. This indeed, as a significant movement of the laity, and a spontaneous movement at that, is one of the most hopeful signs of our time that the goal of our proclamation is being recognized as being nothing less than the redemption of the wilderness, so that all therein "shall see the glory of the Lord, the majesty of our God".

Meanwhile the goal is not yet in sight. The journey through the wilderness may prove to be a short one or a very long-drawn-out process. In either case, lest we faint by the way, God has in fact "spread a table in the wilderness". At this Table the individual, the 'little platoon' and the Great Church are one. It is their real meeting place, indeed the only place where in fact they can all meet. This was symbolized at the beginning of Israel's journey through the wilderness by the eating of the first Passover meal. It was eaten by families, but the individuals who were entitled to eat were also designated, and it was a feast of the whole people. Historically that has been the great unifying

84

symbolic act which more than anything else has kept the people of Israel as an entity all down history. In the history of that other Israel, of which we as Christians are part, the same symbolism is taken by St. Paul and linked to the Lord's Supper, the Holy Communion of the Body and Blood of Christ. It is a notable fact that as St. Paul wrestles with the wilderness experiences of the Corinthian Church (1 *Corinthians* 5. 11) he returns four times in different contexts to the "supernatural food" of the Christian.

I would end this chapter on a note of real urgency. Leaving on one side the tragic fact that this great unifying act of our Lord, the giving to us of his Body and Blood, has, by our sin, been allowed to become a badge of our disunity as Churches, yet surely within each Church it ought to be both the source of unity and therefore the great source of provision for the wilderness. But, so grievous is the shortage of duly appointed representatives of the Church to make available this provision for the way, that for countless Christians to partake of the Holy Communion is a rare event.

This presents one of the most testing of the problems confronting the Church, a problem to which the last Lambeth Conference devoted much attention (see the section on "Man Power and the Ministry") but nevertheless a problem whose full complexity still eludes us. What, for instance, must be the plight of our fellow-Christians in China, scattered far and wide, the vast majority of them out of reach of any regular ministrations of the Church! What is this saying to us? It could pose some very perplexing questions. At least it calls for prayer.

Meanwhile to those of us who can so easily enjoy God's gracious hospitality let us remember that as we

85

do so we are caught up into the mystery of God's sacrifice. For we do not only nourish ourselves. At the same time "we proclaim the Lord's death—until he comes" (1 *Corinthians* 11. 26). Every time we keep the feast we are at once telling the Gospel and moving towards the goal.

E I G H T

THE Bible is a wilderness story. And the first Christian
Martyr, St. Stephen, summarizes the whole story in his
speech for the defence when on trial for his life before
the Council of the Sanhedrin. Vividly he paints the
picture of the Church in the wilderness from Abraham
to the Crucifixion. It is a superb motion picture, as
though it were the very vocation of the Church to be
on the move. Towards the end he speaks of 'the tent
of witness in the wilderness' and then contrasts it with
the Temple in Jerusalem. And he draws this moral.
The 'tent of witness' was a moving tent, ready for
change, ready to go anywhere, to be erected in any
circumstance: in sharpest contrast with a Temple forever fixed in one place, in its nature static, a perpetual
temptation to worshippers to 'settle down'. Was St.
Stephen just making his defence? Surely not. If ever
a man was inviting the death sentence it was he. No,
I believe he was appealing to another audience, to the
Church in Jerusalem, the Church which was already
showing signs of 'settling down', of forgetting its com-
mission to go out to the uttermost parts of the wilderness of the world. It was his great passionate plea that
the Church should remember its Mission. And he did
not plead in vain. The young man who sat consenting
to his death, Saul of Tarsus, never forgot Stephen;

87

his life work, which was to make the Church missionary in the fullest sense of that word, grew out of Stephen's interpretation of the history of God's way of redemption —'in the wilderness prepare'; tell in the wilderness.

This book so far has tried to illustrate one aspect or another of life in the wilderness and of the Gospel to be proclaimed there. We come now to consider in this closing chapter some of the many different methods by which witness to the Gospel is being given today.

But let us begin with one illustration which can sum up much that has gone before. From Sudan comes this salutary challenge to our missionary thinking: "I believe most people still assume that the Africans to whom we missionaries go are like sponges—ready and eager to absorb undiluted all the good teaching and culture we have to impart. It is perhaps interesting to recall that the telegraphic address of the Education Department of the old Sudan Government was 'Instil'. The fact, of course, is that the modern African is far more like a discriminating octopus feeling around in a highly selective manner for what he wants and what he thinks will best nourish him in his search for the knowledge and skill he has decided to acquire. This makes it far more difficult to preach the Gospel—as difficult in fact as it is in the industrialized communities in England." That applies everywhere. Keep it in mind in what follows.

The larger part of the world still consists of village people. We start with them. From Kenya comes this reminder: "If not all Christians are Evangelists, yet all are called to be worshipping witnesses. If the Apostolic ministry included Preaching, Teaching, Fellowship and Worship, then all these things are still essentials of the Christian ministry today. I believe that all these marks of the Christian ministry ought to be present in the *village*. . . . I believe that the Church needs to re-organize itself in a way that will enable us to build up the *Church* in the village, rather than hanging on to the old concept of the church-and-school plot." That is from the Kikuyu country where a vast social revolution is in progress, with the pattern of life completely changed from the days when people lived in scattered households and hamlets. Today the large village, up to ten thousand in population, is the pattern.

The same opportunity is looked at like this from a member of the staff of a theological college in Uganda. "My own view," he says, "would be that as a 'pilot scheme' a member of the Mukono staff should stay in a village for a term at least. . . . Over the period of a year or two each member of the staff should do the same. . . . In so doing the staff would be fitting them-selves for their task of teaching. But more than that, they would be going back into the Church at levels where the ordinary Christian could feel noticed, cared for, and understood" (*A village Church a 'tent of wit-ness'*). . . . "Since in these days God is building up our staff in ways we could not have foreseen, and beyond our hopes, we would, I believe, be only disobedient if we failed to make this deeper identification with the life of the Church at the levels indicated. Quite frankly, I believe this could mean the beginnings of something new and wonderful in the common life of the Church of Uganda."

From the village let us move to the town. This letter comes from a Community Centre in Nairobi: "Effec-tively proclaiming Christ often begins when we meet people at the point of their need; by our supplying the need of which they are conscious, the way is opened for a fuller revelation of the Gospel. Here in Pumwani we have tried to follow this principle in our Community

Centre." He then describes the running of a centre for the children who cannot get into the ordinary schools: coping with teenagers, and especially those who after leaving school are unemployed; providing a meeting place for women different from their drab one-room homes: running a men's club for 'bachelors' whose families are back in the Reserve. "At this stage," he says, "our work may be termed pre-evangelism, and we feel we are digging the soil in which the good seed can be sown." Later he claims for all this no more than that it is "a cup of cold water". But we know our Lord's valuation of that. Here is a real pioneering job in a real wilderness.

The Christian who understands the meaning of healing will have realized that that community centre is a centre of healing. From it let us pass to more traditional methods. A letter from Sierra Leone gives a glimpse of medical work in the villages of the Temne countryside: "The number of patients coming to be treated in one or two of the villages has been exhausting. We have tried to find out why they come when there is a government hospital not so far away. The reply given is to contrast the hospital's atmosphere of noise and impersonality with the village work where each patient is an individual, the work is prayed over at the beginning, and the medicines work. We fully realize that this does not mean thousands pressing into the Kingdom but at least we believe that in a small way witness is being borne to God."

Are Christian hospitals any better? That is a delicate question. So much depends on what you mean by 'better'. But here is a glimpse at two of them. In Northern Nigeria, at Wusasa, is a small hospital in which recently a young woman patient accepted Christ as her Saviour. A doctor writes: "She must have glimpsed that extra something, so difficult to define and so easy to lose, which distinguishes a Christian hospital from others. She had heard the nurses taking prayers in the ward morning by morning. It would appear that she had been most influenced by talking to the nurses. In their compounds the people often gather round in the evening to talk. In a similar way in the wards in the evening, if there is no immediate medical problem, one finds the patients sitting round in a small group talking to the nurses. Some of the nurses had used this opportunity to try to explain the Gospel further to the patients."

These nurses were Africans. What an opportunity is given to the European Sisters who are responsible for training these nurses!

An ordained missionary who is whole-time chaplain to a hospital in Pakistan gives us this insight into his job: "The ground is often hard and stony. The soil needs much breaking up before the seed can take root. For this reason during ward preaching the same story is read and expounded for a week, though a different lesson is brought out daily, the story building up during the week. Humanly speaking we can only expect to scratch the surface during this first encounter. . . . So often in a hospital like ours we are the first link, and will never know when or where the next link may be forged. This we are certain, that if God has been able to forge the first link through the ministry of our hospital, then he will surely provide another link. Then one day someone comes who has heard the Gospel elsewhere, and we have the privilege of being used as a further link. Then again they pass on to some place where there is no Christian testimony. At other times we are allowed the joy of being the 'last link' before their baptism. How very important it is to be faithful

G

links at whatever stage we meet these folk and, like Philip, sensitive to the Spirit's leading."

Are you involved in "link-evangelism"?

A missionary dentist has his moments—not always serious! "One day a man came into the surgery and handed me an old receipt ticket which I had given him for payment of his wife's dentures. 'I want my money back,' he demanded. 'Why, don't they fit?' I asked. 'Oh, it's not that. My wife has run away with another man,' he explained!"

This dentist is running the first mission dental centre in East Africa, and has recently started the first dental service for African schoolchildren in East Africa. There are a surprising number of opportunities for pioneering. At the moment, in addition to everything else, he is coping with 26,000 children "belonging to the Anglican, Roman Catholic and Muslim Missions" in 140 schools. The job, of course, is fantastic. But at this pioneer stage, before the dead hand of bureaucratic routine has taken over, he is free to experiment and has innumerable opportunities. As he says, "a dentist, who believes in the salvation that has been wrought by Jesus Christ, can be greatly used not only by his professional integrity and work, but by his praying, teaching and preaching in the Name of Jesus".

Christian healing is always a co-operative venture—in a very real sense it takes the whole Church to make a man whole. This finds some vivid illustrations from Japan where one of our missionaries tells of several cases where someone she knew was having the best of medical treatment, but was sick in spirit. The medical treatment looked like failing. How often it does when left to itself! In one case the 'demon' of worry had to be cast out, and a home made available at any time for the worried man to find peace. He found it, and then highly specialized medical skill was able to complete his cure. In another case of desperate illness the Gospel which can make a man every whit whole added just the necessary ingredient to family devotion and medical skill. "Medical attention, loving nursing and prayer brought him through the illness and grateful as they are to the doctor they know that God himself is the greater Physician."

Every doctor and every nurse was once either a schoolboy or a schoolgirl. In the missionary enterprise that is something we have always known. Out from Christian schools go the boys and girls who are to be doctors and nurses, and leaders in every branch of the common life. In days when many of the opportunities provided by the one-time Christian monopoly of education have disappeared it is good to read these words from an Indian headmaster of a Christian school in Bengal. "The door of presenting Christ through institutions is still open. People are eager to hear of our Lord and of his teaching. Bible teaching is no longer compulsory in our schools, ours being a secular State, and yet not a single boy at St. John's absents himself from the Bible classes. The sons of professors, police superintendents, the district inspector of schools, the district magistrate, etc., all are there learning of Jesus as their fathers did before them, although they are not Christians. Good will is spreading and I believe that the harvest is getting ripe for the reaping."

From Jordan comes this brief observation with a wealth of wisdom concealed in it. "The Gospel is certainly proclaimed through much English literature that is read and taught. In a Christian school all such literature chosen and taught—and very much enjoyed by staff and girls—can be effective." She adds, "the teaching of Scripture to all Christian denominations from kindergarten to the top class is an ever-present opportunity".

In that school Muslim children are not allowed to attend the Scripture classes. But they are absorbing 'English Literature'. Have we reflected that the English language, like other European languages, was formed in its critical early stages under the continual impact of the Christian Church and the Christian Gospel, as were none of the other great languages of the world? That is an enormously significant fact in a world which is having to learn English as its 'second language'. And 'English Literature' is a vital part of the learning of English. And English literature is unintelligible without a knowledge of the Bible, without some understanding of the Christian faith. Does that open up vistas? It ought to!

Schools, as I suggested above, are in these days often very closely linked up with the ministry of healing. A common link between them is the attempt to deal with malnutrition which is the predisposing cause of so much ill-health. Preventive medicine is best practised at school. I quote from a letter from Uganda, describing an experiment of this kind in which the World Health Organization has shown the greatest interest. "Our Society sent a woman farmer and dietician and we had an African teacher who had some knowledge of dietetics, and the experiment began. A new girl coming into the school for six years shares in work on the farm learning new ways . . . in the school dining-room the food from the farm is varied and tasty and she sees girls, longer in the school, eager to eat new things, even to break old taboos. Later she will learn the *why* of it all. Thus we believe we are working with girls some of whom, at least, will not be content until they have brought these changes into their own homes and villages. And all this is brought into the school chapel, to be prayed for, given thanks for, brought back to be laid at the feet of the One who loves and cares for the whole man, spirit, mind and body." A wilderness of malnutrition becoming 'a garden of the Lord'—men and women in a new way understanding 'the majesty of our God'.

A very large part of the missionary contribution to education today consists in the training of teachers, the creation of a Christian teaching profession, one that operates not only in Church schools but throughout the whole educational system of the country. That is the vision which appears in this letter from South India. "The role of the teacher, once he has got his Christian teaching principles clear, is to bear witness among his fellow-teachers, only after that among the students. We need far more teachers in government schools who will labour away for higher standards of teaching, for a nobler conception of the teacher's profession."

In the wilderness of so much education in which the pressures on the teachers are so often intolerable there is a wonderful Christian opportunity for witness and for training others to be witnesses in this particular bit of the wilderness of our time.

Education, however, is not just an affair of schools, training colleges, or even universities. There is the whole vast—and as yet hardly touched—field of adult education; offering to the Christian Church, in some ways, its greatest opportunity today, and calling for an almost infinite variety of approach. One such approach was tried more than a generation ago in Japan with great effect through newspaper evangelism. Today correspondence courses seem to offer a wide-open door of opportunity. It is certainly being taken in Iran; and through the initiative of an American missionary at

Vellore in South India, thousands of non-Christians are being reached and, when it is properly followed up at the local level, it results in conversions to Christ. That is just one door which is ajar and only needs pushing.

Most of the illustrations so far, though not all, have shown the infinite variety of proclamation possible from some institution as its base, if that institution is once seen to be, as it can be, 'a tent in the wilderness' and not a static unmovable shrine. 'Mobility' is one of our most urgent needs in the missionary movement. But that does not mean supersonic air travel. It means an attitude of mind which is always 'going out', which knows that the horizon is only the limit of our sight, that always "there is something lost behind the ranges, something waiting" and which knows that it must obey the command to 'go'.

Let us look now at another range of witness. A good bridge can be made from institutional life to other kinds of living by this letter from an institution in Sierra Leone. "We have noticed that time and time again," writes this missionary, "old students do not comment on their lectures, the college services and so on, it is always our home and our children that seem to have spoken to their hearts, and stirred a longing for something they have never known. It is in the home that we are most conscious of being used."

The home naturally leads us on to consider the openings for witness of the layman going about his ordinary everyday business. We are certainly going to see much more of this in every country. Here is a report of what one of our missionaries sees happening in South India. "I could hardly close without a word about the 'new pattern' of the Church in India. The idea of paid agents of the Gospel is foreign to both Hindus and Muslims. We constantly hear the remark

'Oh, but he is paid to preach his religion'. Christ will be far more effectively preached in forward evangelism by dedicated voluntary workers than by paid catechists, teachers, or even pastors. We are working at this centre for a 'Lay Apostolate', a body of lay people who will proclaim Christ through a medium acceptable to the people of this land. We get some very fine people here, literate villagers who are the salt of the earth. Devoid of inhibitions, they can learn very quickly the principles of the proclamation of the Gospel."

The transition to the next sphere of witness may appear a little sudden. But it takes all sorts to make a world. And the wilderness certainly includes prisons! And there have been some notable Christian prisoners. One thinks of Paul, of Bunyan, and more recently of Clutton-Brock in Southern Rhodesia. So why should we be surprised to hear from Ruanda of a young man, upon whom his Christian schooling had made only a faint impression, and who was converted while in prison by the preaching of a visiting African pastor. Out of that prison (a wilderness experience on any reckoning) he wrote these words: "Here in the prison Jesus has helped me to overcome fear and to preach the Gospel. Already five of those with me in prison have received the Lord Jesus and had the courage to witness for him." I like the way he ends: "And let us not despair; there will be more." The 'tent of witness' is thoroughly mobile!

In Colombo it has been erected in a Singhalese rector's study. There he has dealt, in recent years, with a number of Buddhists who wished to marry Christian girls. He has never started by preaching the Gospel to them or pressing them to accept baptism. Instead he expounded the Christian doctrine of marriage, with its teaching about the sacramental nature

97

of the physical. This comes as an entirely new revelation to Buddhists brought up to believe that both matter and desire are evil and that salvation can only be attained by escaping from both. And he has found that in no less than six cases recently this has opened the door and eventually the young man has asked for baptism.

Another very important way of Christian witness is through co-operation with non-Christians. In Iran it may be making the Christian hospital available for training government nurses, responding to the request of the Chancellor of the University. "I want you to train them in your hospital. I want these girls to know what Christian nursing really is." In Northern Nigeria it may take the form of joining in the local branch of the R.S.P.C.A. and in that 'neutral' activity finding that "doors have been opened in the wall between Muslims and Christians". In East Africa it may be through extending an invitation to a Pakistani Muslim missionary to come to those lectures being given to a group of ordinands on Islam so that he can "challenge my presentation where necessary, supplement it, and enter freely into discussion with the students. In these days when there is a determined advance of Islam in East Africa, such links are not to be despised. At the very least they serve to allay any suspicion that we are teaching in a prejudiced way. At best they are a beginning of the Gospel, maybe".

We Christians have a wonderful opportunity for proclaiming the universal Christ when we can show him transcending barriers of race and denomination. It was interesting to read of a primary school in Malaya whose staff consists of two Indians, two Chinese and two Malays—one being an Anglican, one a Mar Thoma, two Methodists and two Muslims. A glimpse of the same possibility comes from Ceylon where a missionary can write of the Christian Church: "We are the only body in Ceylon that embraces all communities. The Buddhists are all Singhalese, and the Hindus all Tamil, and the Muslims all North Indian or Malay, but in the Christian Church alone are there both Tamils and Singhalese" and, incidentally, Europeans.

I wish it were possible to write of Christian unity as a 'witness in the wilderness'. Perhaps we will serve the cause best by being honest and admitting that despite 'South India', despite 'plans' of Church Union elsewhere, despite many co-operative institutions and joint centres for theological training, and much sincere seeking to know and understand one another better in the ecumenical movement, we Christians are still in this respect making a wilderness of the Garden of the Lord.

Because that thought should drive us to prayer and to action I can best close this chapter with an illustration of almost unlimited application. Incidentally it is a good illustration of missionaries and Christians in 'secular' employment getting together. "It is a long way," says the writer of this letter, "from Lee Abbey in North Devon to Enugu in Eastern Nigeria. Yet what is being done in Lee Abbey is having its effect out here. A government official and his wife were transferred to an appointment in Enugu. After they had been here a few weeks they came to me and asked if they could share in prayer some of the burdens and problems of our Church life. The two of them and my wife and myself arranged to meet together once each week for prayer and fellowship and quiet waiting upon God. Whilst on leave in England our two friends had visited Lee Abbey and there had been introduced to the idea of 'the Christian cell in the parish'. The four of us met regularly each week, sharing in prayer our problems, personal and parochial. Our fellowship together was a great encouragement to us. After a time we invited others to join us and we now number fourteen in all. This number is too big for one group, so we have split into two groups. We have seen wonderful things happen—we have seen sick people recover— lapsed Christians brought back into the fellowship of the Church—a husband and wife converted—strained relationships redeemed—and who knows what will happen next?"

In the wilderness we never do know what will happen next beyond the certainty that *anywhere* it is possible to pitch 'the tent of witness', together with the equal certainty that wherever we pitch it we will meet God.

There are those who are saying that the day of the foreign missionary is over. I hope this chapter will have shown that they are wrong.

Epilogue

As Moses lifted up the serpent in the wilderness, so must the Son of man be lifted up . . . for God so loved the world that he gave his only Son, that whoever believes in him should not perish but have eternal life.   ST. JOHN 3. 14, 16

WEST AFRICA, East Africa, Sudan and the Middle East, Iran and Pakistan, India and Ceylon, Malaya and Japan, not to mention China, and her window of Hong Kong—all these have contributed towards the picture of that wilderness of our age which this book has attempted to portray, and of which we in Britain, in Europe, the Americas and Australasia are most surely a part.

One overwhelming impression remains from all the many letters I have received from so many places, and that is of the things we all share in common. The differences between countries and nations and races and circumstances are nothing like as remarkable as the similarities.

It falls to my lot very frequently to travel by road from Blackheath to Blackfriars. I am quite familiar with that bit of the wilderness of South London! In the course of various journeys I have also travelled by road from Freetown to Port Loko, from Kano to Lagos, from Onitsha to Port Harcourt, from Dar-es-Salaam to Morogoro and Dodoma. I know the road from Nairobi to Kisumu over the Rift Valley. I have driven from Kampala to Gulu, and from Juba to Yambio. I know the road from Cairo to Menouf, the road from

Kowloon to the border of China, and even some of the roads round Shanghai and Hangchow and Nanking, to say nothing of American 'thruways' and German autobahns. I can only testify from my own experience that the people who live beside the road from Blackheath to Blackfriars are very like the people who frequent other roads. To begin with I've found them all likeable, all about equally suspicious of strangers, all equally ready to join in a joke and to share a smile—all of them children of God. But I've not gone about with my eyes shut. I've seen where they lived, studied something of their problems, seen a little below the surface of their lives, and found there, in every case, the same common needs.

If, as I hope, I some day see the Grand Trunk Road from Calcutta to Delhi, watch the road from Peshawar disappearing up the Khyber Pass to Kabul, drive up into the mountains from Tokyo, travel from Kuala Lumpur to Ipoh, and go down from Jerusalem to Jericho—and fulfil a lot of other dreams, I have no doubt whatever that I shall find men and women just as likeable as I've found them on the roads I know already. And I doubt not that they'll be facing much the same problems, and deep down there will be the same tremendous needs.

When we really get down below our superficial differences we know with St. Paul that the truth about us all is that "there is no distinction; since all have sinned and fall short of the glory of God" (*Romans* 3. 23). We are all in the wilderness without exception. But that isn't the last word. St. Paul goes on to say that "they (that is all of us) are justified by his grace through the redemption which is in Christ Jesus" (v. 24). In the wilderness is the sign of the Cross.

Are we prepared to meet there, and, like that

African whose story closed Chapter VI, be broken at the foot of the Cross, and then rise to share the redeeming power of the crucified and risen Son of God?

Let this book's final message come from a missionary who might be any missionary, perhaps any committed Christian anywhere. "Since coming here my wife and I have begun to feel just a little of the weight of the Cross, to experience ourselves just a little of what it cost to redeem the world. In the Gospels we read of the crowds which pressed around the Lord, so that he had not time even to eat; of the crying of the multitudes with their sicknesses, failures, sins and other needs; of the infinite demand which confronted him every hour of every day. So we ourselves are presented with the demands of the hungry and ragged children, the scabies, ulcers and stomach-aches, and all the people wanting this or that, invading our privacy, keeping us from our food and rest. As the multitudes felt that they had the right to what our Lord had for the relief of their necessity; as some would not take 'No' for an answer, like the Syro-Phoenician woman, and would go to any lengths to get what they wanted, like the men who broke up the roof where Jesus was: so it is to a lesser extent with us. What the Lord had was the power to heal, what we have in the eyes of the people around us is worldly possessions. To help anyone costs something in time, in money, in energy, and to these there is a limit. Even for our Lord there was a limit to his time and physical strength, and from time to time he was forced to turn his back on the crowds. For instance, I may from time to time be able to help in bringing a very sick man into hospital from a village thirty miles away. I cannot possibly undertake to run an ambulance service for the whole of my district. For every one helped there are many left without help.

"But where there is compassion, the true charity which suffers with the sufferer, when someone seeks our help, we must necessarily feel the pain of their affliction, whether we can help them or not. And the pain will be in direct proportion to our charity. We dare not harden our hearts and shut out charity, yet we cannot help all who ask for help. We can only learn to love and to suffer and to know the length and breadth and depth and height of the love of Christ, who bore in his own body the sorrows of the world."

There is just one rule for the wilderness trail—

Measure thy life by loss instead of gain
Not by the wine drunk but the wine poured forth
For love's strength standeth in love's sacrifice
And he who suffers most has most to give[1]

So, upon the Son of Man lifted up we fix our gaze. So looking we have all that we need for the story we have to tell in the wilderness.

[1] From the poem "The Disciples", by Harriet Eleanor Hamilton Smith (Kegan Paul, 1916), p. 91.

Are YOU "telling in the wilderness"?

*

Are you:

> learning to think and act in a Christian way towards people of other races? (page 10)

> "building the bridge" across denominational divisions? (page 14)

> welcoming overseas visitors into your parish, into your home? (page 51)

> giving thanks for the faithful prayer of others for the growth of the Kingdom and being faithful in prayer yourself? (page 54)

> willing to be used as one small, perhaps unknown, bit of "link-evangelism"? (page 91)

> ready to be "broken at the foot of the Cross, and then rise to share the redeeming power of the crucified and risen Son of God"? (page 103)

If you have found the freely flowing grace of God in the wilderness of your own life, are you now committed to helping others find that grace? One way of affirming such a commitment is to become a Registered Member of the Church Missionary Society. Through its fellowship of prayer, of service and of giving, you can share in the task of "telling in the wilderness".

Are YOU a Registered Member of C.M.S.? If not, write for the free Membership leaflet to:

THE HOME SECRETARY
C.M.S., 6 SALISBURY SQUARE, LONDON E.C.4.